WELWYN'S RAILWAYS

Plate 1 (Frontispiece) *BR Class 9F 2–10–0 No 92148 passing Welwyn North station on an up mixed-goods train on 18 July 1959*   © *D. E. White*

WELWYN'S RAILWAYS

A History of the Great Northern Line from 1850 to 1986

The Reverend Tom W. Gladwin

Peter W. Neville

and

Douglas E. White

'Nowhere can I think so happily as in a train'.

A. A. MILNE
From *If I May* (London 1921)

CASTLEMEAD PUBLICATIONS

WARE

First Published in 1986

CASTLEMEAD PUBLICATIONS
Swains Mill, 4A Crane Mead
Ware, Herts., SG12 9PY

Publishing division of
WARD'S PUBLISHING SERVICES

British Library Cataloguing in Publication Data

Gladwin, Thomas William
    Welwyn's railways: a history of the Great
    Northern Line from 1850–1986.
    1. Railroads—England—Welwyn Region
    (Hertfordshire)—History
    I. Title   II. Neville, Peter W.   III. White,
    Douglas E.
    385'.09425'86   HE3019.W3/

    ISBN 0–948555–04–1

Printed in Great Britain
in 10pt Palatino Roman Type
by Anchor Brendon Limited, Tiptree, Essex

Preface

This book has its origins in a small booklet *Welwyn North: The Story of the Railway* (Gladwin, Neville & White. 1985) produced to coincide with a railway exhibition and lectures in Digswell Village Hall, close to Welwyn North station, on 22 February 1985. However, limitations of space meant that much available information had to be excluded from that very restricted account which, as stated, was intended to form the basis of a more detailed publication. Thus, also greatly encouraged by many requests for the promised larger, illustrated and more comprehensive account, we continued our researches and this book is the product of that work.

As with the earlier booklet, preparation of the present work has been a somewhat difficult task. In particular we have been greatly concerned to resolve discrepancies in earlier manuscript material which have often been repeated by other dependent authors. It is our hope that any errors in the present work are minimal.

We have generally remained true to the conventions and standards adopted in the source manuscripts used in the production of the present work. Thus, the station name Welwyn is retained in those parts of the account which refer to the period up to 1926 when it was changed to Welwyn North. Similarly am and pm have been used until 1965 when British Railways adopted the 24-hour clock.

Imperial measurements are also used where appropriate. British Railways Working Timetables, for example, continue to show distances in miles and chains (1 mile = 80 chains) and the standard gauge continues to be quoted as 4 ft 8½ in. Similarly fares are given in the currency in which they were originally quoted. Decimalisation of sterling, which established the relationship between the former and present currencies of 240d ('old' pennies) equals 100p (new pence), occurred in 1972.

Rev. Tom Gladwin
Peter Neville
Douglas White

Digswell, May 1986

Acknowledgements

We acknowledge with grateful thanks the assistance and information we have received from many sources. In particular we have been privileged to have had much support and advice from Eric Neve who subscribed the bulk of the chapters on *Express Trains*, *Motive Power* and *Goods and Mineral*, and unselfishly checked a large part of our complete typescript. His considerable knowledge of Great Northern Railway history and meticulous concern for accuracy resulted in many improvements to our original manuscript. John Aylard kindly provided the chapter on *Coaching Stock* and Geoff Woodward a detailed account of signalling on which the chapter, *Signals and Signalling*, is based. David Elsdon, the present manager of *The Cowper Arms* at Digswell, subscribed the chapter of that title. For assistance in obtaining and providing information we are also grateful to Monica Coleman, V. H. Cutts, the late Dorothy Day, Christopher Duffell, Terry Henderson, Mrs Shelagh Head of Hertfordshire County Library, the Hertfordshire County Records Office, Dr Christine Johnstone (Curator of the Welwyn Hatfield Museum Service), the late Cyril King, Keith A. Ladbury, the National Railway Museum Library, and R. Temple. We are equally grateful to Miss Elspeth Marshall for assistance in providing word processing facilities and producing most of the final typescript, Peter Davies for obtaining the fine aerial view of Digswell Viaduct, Stephen Bayley for the artwork for maps and plans, Ronald Maddox for the fine jacket design, and all who kindly gave permission for the reproduction of their photographs.

All known sources have been acknowledged and we apologise for the few instances where they could not be traced.

Our railways have given us, the writers, much pleasure over many years. Although, as in any organisation, things may not always run as planned, we remain great admirers of British Railways' efficient operation of its complex and intricate network. We are also appreciative of the many benefits and improvements due to the continuing huge capital investment in modernisation. More especially, on behalf of all who use Welwyn North station, we are pleased to record our gratitude to British Railways staff for their many courtesies.

List of Colour Plates

Contents

List of Illustrations

Bookjacket

'The Flying Scotsman' heading north over Digswell Viaduct in the 1930s.
The viewpoint is from the drive of Tewin Water House. An especially
commissioned painting by Ronald Maddox VPRI, FSIAD, FSAI.

List of Tables

Abbreviations

BR	British Rail	HST	InterCity 125 High Speed Train
CME	Chief Mechanical Engineer	LMR	London Midland Region
DMU	Diesel Multiple Unit	LMS	London Midland & Scottish Railway
ECML	East Coast Main Line	LNER	London & North Eastern Railway
EMU	Electric Multiple Unit	LNWR	London & North Western Railway
GCR	Great Central Railway	SECR	South Eastern & Chatham Railway
GER	Great Eastern Railway	SR	Southern Railway or
GNR	Great Northern Railway		Southern Region after 1948
GWR	Great Western Railway	WR	Western Region

Chapter 1

Introduction

Most of Hertfordshire's towns and villages are well served by main line railways to five London termini and inner suburban services to Moorgate. From Kings Cross the Great Northern line with its subsidiary loop via Hertford North serves a third of the population of the county. This book sets out to record a history of the GN line at Welwyn from its inception in 1850 to May 1986, when work to extend the electrification of the railway from Hitchin to Leeds and Edinburgh is proceeding rapidly. The new electric train services are planned to be introduced in stages between 1987 and 1990.

Welwyn has always occupied a prominent place in the history of the railway. The station, opened in 1850 to serve the larger village 1½ miles distant, actually lies within the ecclesiastical Parish of Digswell, a name the station might well have borne had it not been for the well known coaching village of Welwyn on the Great North Road.

However, Digswell is a very special railway village. It is set in a beautiful wooded valley landscape, enhanced by its famous railway viaduct. Together with the two tunnels and one of the few remaining largely unspoilt Great Northern Railway stations

(renamed Welwyn North in 1926), the railway through Digswell bears witness to the great architectural and engineering achievements of the early Victorian period.

Known locally as the 'east coast bottleneck' because of the limitations imposed by the reduction from four to two tracks between Digswell Junction and Woolmer Green, the railway here has a unique and fascinating history. During its 136 years of operation it has undergone many great changes. Some are the consequence of the technical development of the railway itself. Others, however, are due to its serving an increasing population attracted largely by the mobility it continues to afford.

Digswell is largely a product of the railway; few residents are unaffected by it and many moved there because of it. For many it provides the necessary means for getting to and from their places of employment. For train spotting schoolboys and many adults it is a source of pleasure. For photographers such as G. W. Goslin, and artists such as W. Humber, S. R. Badmin, and Ronald Maddox who lives in Digswell, it is a source of inspiration and self-expression.

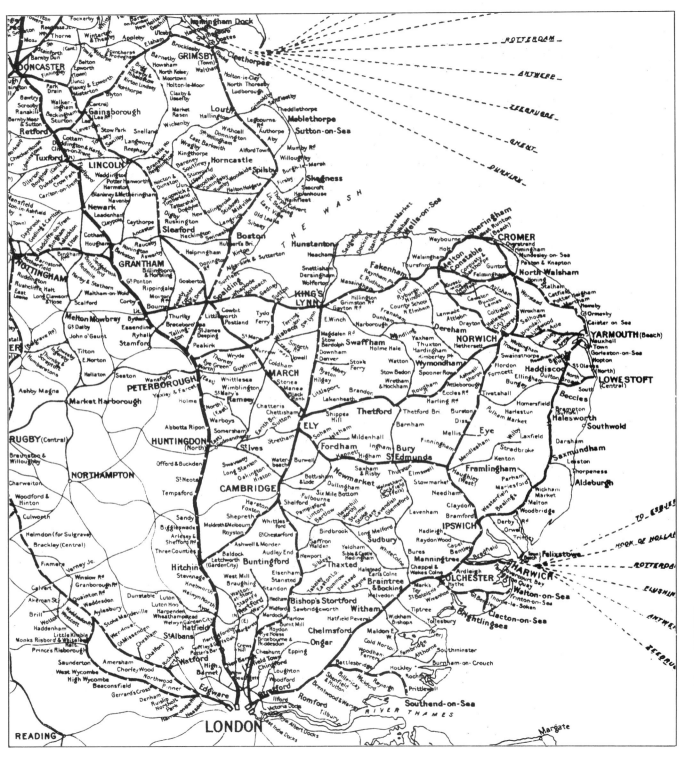

Figure 1.1 *Part of the official map*
London and North Eastern Railway and
Connecting Railways *published in 1930 by George
Philip & Sons Ltd.*

12

Chapter 2

A Short History of Railways Around Welwyn

The first plans for a railway through Welwyn were deposited in 1845 in the name of the Bedfordshire, Hertfordshire and Essex Junction Railway. The proposals were to construct a line which, *en route* from Luton to Harlow, would have passed through Ayot St Lawrence, Welwyn village and along the Mimram valley under the site of Digswell Viaduct and on through Tewin Lower Green. The scheme failed because of a lack of financial support.

Parliamentary assent to the construction of a railway between London and York was granted on 26 June 1846, on which date the Great Northern Railway was incorporated.

2.1 The Great Northern Railway

Edmund Denison was responsible for the scheme to connect London and York by rail and William Cubitt, the consulting engineer, was responsible for the final survey of the line. The route, too well known to be detailed here, resulted in Welwyn (or more appropriately Digswell), twenty-two miles from London, being directly served by a railway. Building of the railway from London to Peterborough commenced in 1848, with Joseph Cubitt, son of William, as the resident engineer.

It was not an easy line to construct, there being no fewer than nine tunnels in the first 23½ miles from Kings Cross to Woolmer Green and, of course, the famous Digswell Viaduct. Thomas Brassey obtained the contract for the construction of the line from Peterborough to Copenhagen Tunnel (Holloway). The temporary terminus at Maiden Lane was built by John Jay who also completed the line from there to Kings Cross. Copenhagen Tunnel was constructed by Pearce and Smith. As the technology of curved tunnels had not then been perfected, all nine tunnels between Woolmer Green, Welwyn and London

are straight. The two Welwyn tunnels are on a straight section of track anyway, but between Potters Bar and Hadley Wood the line is curved all the way, except through the tunnels.

Grinling (1898) in his *History of the Great Northern Railway* states,

> The directors, characteristically, decided not to put the Company to the expenses of festivities to celebrate the opening but they did not refuse an invitation which Mr Brassey issued to them, and to some four hundred others, to take a trial trip on the line on 5 August 1850 – two days before the public working began. It is also reported that this train, comprising two engines and seventeen carriages, left at 9 am and after several stops, including one 'to enable passengers to descend to the Mimram Valley and obtain a good view of the splendid viaduct', arrived at Peterborough just after 1.30 pm.

The first public train, a Parliamentary one required to call at all stations, departed from the temporary station at Maiden Lane at 6 am on Wednesday 7 August 1850 and would have called at Welwyn, now Welwyn North, although the station was only partially built at the time. Regular passenger services to York started on the following day.

The line from Kings Cross to Woolmer Green was a hard one for the steam locomotives. As the line leaves Kings Cross there is an up gradient of 1 in 107 under Gasworks and Copenhagen Tunnels, and a continuous gradient of 1 in 200 for the eight-mile stretch from Wood Green to Potters Bar. Thence to Woolmer Green the line is undulating with a final rise of 1 in 200/330. (*See* Figure 2.2.)

With the inception of diesel locomotive haulage in 1958 and the present diesel-electric powered High Speed Trains, little trouble is experienced in the initial section from Kings Cross and the often heavily loaded inner and outer suburban electric services make light work of the gradients.

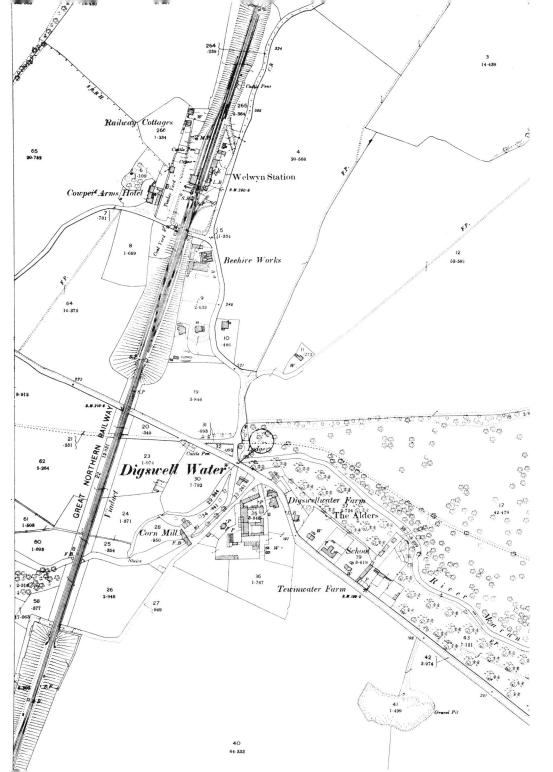

In the days of steam haulage there were various proposals to widen the section from Welwyn Garden City to Woolmer Green from two to four tracks. The cost of widening Digswell Viaduct and the duplication of Welwyn South (447 yards) and North (1047 yards) Tunnels, formerly Lockleys Hill and Harmer Green Tunnels respectively, put paid to these proposals. Today, with careful timetable planning and the demise of slow moving freight trains, together with the availability of the alternative route between Wood Green and Stevenage via Cuffley and Hertford North, the original two-track layout suffices. The estimated cost of a new line from Enfield to Stevenage in 1898 was £1.25 m, but it was considered that this scheme would generate more traffic than widening to four tracks the two-track sections between Greenwood and Potters Bar and Digswell Junction to Woolmer Green at a lesser cost of £800 000 (Young 1977).

2.2 Welwyn Junction station

The first railway station in what is now Welwyn Garden City was opened in 1858 to serve as an interchange enabling passengers using the Hertford and Welwyn Junction Railway trains to join down main line trains. Known as Welwyn Junction station it comprised two platforms and was situated to the north of the present Welwyn Garden City station, but it was closed on 1 September 1860 when the Welwyn Junction to Luton section of the Dunstable branch opened and Hatfield became the interchange station for both branch lines. Trains from Hertford and Dunstable then joined the double-track main line at Welwyn Junction (to terminate at Hatfield) until separate tracks to Hatfield were opened in 1868. These comprised a single Dunstable line on the west side of the double-track main line and a single Hertford line on the east side. Welwyn Junction station was subsequently demolished.

Figure 2.1   A section of an Ordnance Survey map published in 1898 showing the GNR through Welwyn   Courtesy of Hertfordshire County Record Office

Stations shown thus – **HATFIELD**   Signal Boxes shown vertically thus – **REDHALL**

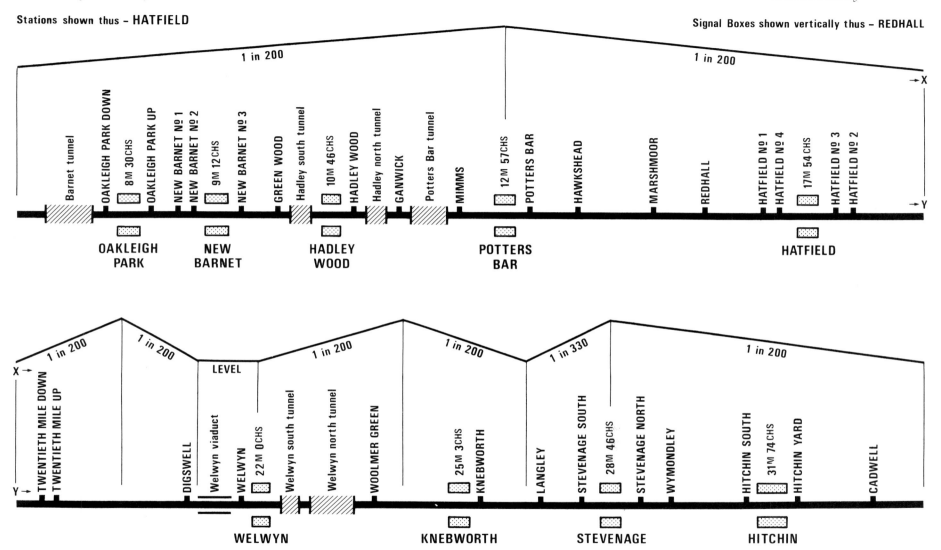

Figure 2.2   *Diagram showing the gradient profile and distances on the GNR from Kings Cross to Hitchin*

In 1917 halt platforms were erected on both the Dunstable and Hertford branches, immediately north of Hunter's Bridge. These were for the sole use of railway employees. On 16 August 1920 the platform on the Dunstable branch, developed by the provision of timber-built station buildings, was opened to passengers with access from Hunter's Bridge, and thus became the predecessor to the present station at Welwyn Garden City. As to the station's inclusion in the timetables, quite properly there is no reference to it in July 1920. However in the appropriate November timetables of that year a footnote reference says 'Calls at a *Halt* at Welwyn Garden City between Hatfield and Ayot'. There were then five down trains and three in the up

Figure 2.3 *Welwyn station looking south, c.1860–70. Note the clay ballast, low platforms and absence of footbridge*

Figure 2.4 *Welwyn station looking north at the turn of the century. Note the ballast and preparations for the cattle sidings*   © *Welwyn Times*

direction each weekday. By August 1926, immediately prior to the opening of the present station, the 'Halt' was served by seventeen down and sixteen up trains per weekday, which indicates the growth of Welwyn Garden City. At this time a train referred to in the timetable as the 'Garden City Express' left Kings Cross at 10.55 am and after calling at Finsbury Park ran non-stop to the 'Halt' arriving at 11.30 am. The Express returned at 5.33 pm and after the Finsbury Park stop arrived at Kings Cross at 6.5 pm. Nameboards erected on the station were lettered Welwyn Garden City with no reference to its status as a Halt.

Photographs of the wooden platform on the Hertford branch suggest it never carried a name board and, unlike Attimore Halt on the same branch, it was never shown in the public timetables as a stop for passenger services. It therefore seems safe to assume that it was indeed solely for the use of railway employees. It was presumably dismantled at the same time as the Luton line platform. The opening of the present station to passengers on 20 September 1926 was followed by the formal opening by the Rt. Hon. Neville Chamberlain on 5 October 1926. The new station included separate platform faces for Hertford and Dunstable branch trains.

As the existence of the GNR main line at Welwyn influenced those wishing to create a second garden city (the first was at Letchworth) it is appropriate to trace the history of this development in relation to the railway.

2.3 Welwyn Garden City

Land for the creation of the new garden city was purchased in 1919 and one of the first tasks of the Resident Engineer, Captain W. E. James RE, was to plan a comprehensive 2 ft-gauge railway system to avoid the need to rely on existing farm tracks for the transport of building materials.

At that time the nearest GNR good yards were at Ayot and Hatfield, but there was also a 5-wagon length farm siding on the Luton branch servicing Handside Farm. The siding in question was known as Horn's Siding after the occupant of the farm. Captain James quickly enlarged this siding to accommodate forty wagons, from which bricks and other building materials could be off-loaded onto horse-drawn carts, until the narrow gauge railway was completed. It is recorded that the first consignment of bricks was taken to a housing site in Handside Lane on 26 April 1920. At about this time Trollope & Colls Ltd were appointed contractors by Welwyn Garden City Ltd and gradually the narrow gauge line was developed to connect with Horn's Siding. Sandpits and a brickworks were established near Sandpit Bridge, which crossed the main line railway until it was demolished during electrification of the main line in the 1970s. The largest pit, which supplied the bulk of material for a number of years, was at Twentieth Mile and there were smaller pits in Brockswood Lane and Valley Road. The narrow gauge railway

connected these installations with Horn's Siding and, as required, new tracks were laid to the development sites as building progressed.

In 1924 a new gravel pit was opened at Digswell Water and the narrow gauge railway was extended there to transport gravel to the Twentieth Mile plant for washing.

Trollope & Colls' contract ended in 1923 and thereafter all construction was carried out by Welwyn Builders Ltd, a subsidiary of the development company. The narrow gauge railway continued to be operated by the new owners, but as the town developed, so the need for it lessened and by the early 1930s only the line from the Digswell Water Pit to the Twentieth Mile plant remained. This eventually closed in

Figure 2.5 Welwyn Garden City station in 1920 showing the platform on the Luton branch (left) and the Hertford branch platform © *E. J. Miller*

1936/7. During its existence the railway was operated by four-wheeled 20 hp petrol locomotives, all built by Motor Rail of Bedford. One 40 hp locomotive was also provided for the haul up from the Digswell Water Pit to the plateau on which the ICI complex was subsequently built. Another line which should be mentioned was that from Twentieth Mile Bridge to the New Town Agricultural Guild's Model Dairy at Handside Farm in Handside Lane which removed manure from the farm to the nursery garden in Brockswood Lane (Digswell Nurseries).

Figure 2.6 *The original station at Welwyn Garden City on the Luton branch in 1921. Note the GNR timetables, the recently built GNR Class N2 0–6–2T No 1760 and the Twentieth Mile signal box distant somersault signal in the background*
© *R. C. Pakes*

2.4 Welwyn Garden City station

When the present main line station was opened in 1926 the population of Welwyn Garden City was 4500 but the station had been planned for a ten-fold increase of this figure, the population duly reaching 47 000 in 1978.

The main station building at the east end of Howardsgate is of the neo-Georgian style (*see* Figure 2.8) which was adopted for the Garden City and designed by the chief architect to the development company, Louis de Soissons. It was built mainly of local red brick, probably from a brickworks established near present-day Burrowfield, the portico of the entrance being of terra-cotta with a reinforced concrete roof. The station consists of two island platforms each 600 feet long, of which 150 feet is roofed over, the roof being constructed of spare materials assembled by the London & North Eastern Railway at various places. One island platform served all the down stopping trains as well as both directions of the Hatfield–Luton and Dunstable service. This is now the main platform for the electric trains to and from Moorgate. The other platform accommodated the up stopping trains and both directions of the Hatfield–Hertford service. (*See* Figure 2.9.)There are substantial red brick buildings on both island platforms, comprising waiting rooms, staff rooms and toilets, and from time to time the platforms have been embellished with well tended rose and flower beds. Access to the platforms from the ticket hall is by a footbridge which was extended in 1936 to provide both an access to the station from the east side (Hyde Way) and as a short cut to the town centre on the purchase of a platform ticket. This toll was abolished in the early 1980s. There are no platform faces for the main lines which run through the centre of the station. An extensive goods yard was provided, one of its main customers being the Shredded Wheat Company (now Nabisco) and there were additional sidings for stabling empty passenger trains. (*See* Figure 2.10.)

As the development of Welwyn Garden City proceeded, so

Plate 2 *An aerial view of Digswell showing the viaduct in 1986*   © *Peter Davies*

more of the inner suburban services were progressively extended out to it. This in itself brought operating problems as all down trains terminating at Welwyn Garden City to form trains returning south had to cross all the main tracks and reverse into the up platform. Following this, the locomotives of these trains had to 'run round' and be attached to the front of the train. In busy periods this was a difficult operation but although delays to other services occurred, there is no record of any accident happening as a result of these train movements. Two major accidents have occurred at Welwyn Garden City (in 1935 and 1957) which, together with other lesser accidents, are described in Chapter 12. With the electrification of the inner

Figure 2.7   The original Welwyn Garden City station prior to closure in 1926. Note the new signals installed in connection with the new station and signal box opened later that year   © R. C. Pakes

suburban services in 1976 the track layouts were revised and a north-west/south-east single-track flyover was erected south of the station enabling terminated down trains to depart southbound without obstructing the main line. By then passenger services had long ceased to Luton and Dunstable (24 April 1965) and to Hertford (18 June 1951) and nine carriage sidings with carriage washing facilities were constructed to the north of the station.

Currently there is a half-hourly weekday service all day from Welwyn Garden City to Kings Cross and Letchworth (hourly to Royston), and a twenty-minute all-stations service to Moorgate; there are variations during peak periods and on Sundays. Driver-only operation of the inner suburban trains, which commenced in late 1985, was due for completion in 1986. The original goods station at Welwyn Garden City was closed, and in 1985 the site was let by British Rail to UMB Freights (Welwyn) Ltd which operates a Freight Terminal Depot with full rail access. This was formally opened by the Chairman of the Welwyn Hatfield District Council, Councillor J. McDonald, on 28 January 1986.

UMB has obtained a contract from Pedigree Petfoods of Melton Mowbray which will utilise a large proportion of the 103 000 square feet of covered warehousing as a main southern distribution point for their products. The first consignment from Melton Mowbray of a million cans of pet food arrived for the opening ceremony behind Class 47 locomotive No. 47 280 which had been specially named *Pedigree* at a ceremony at Melton Mowbray the previous day. During May 1986 the original brick built goods shed was demolished.

The outward appearance of the station has remained basically unchanged since 1926 and has begun to look neglected and in need of refurbishment. However in February 1985 a planning application (C6/108/85) was made to the Welwyn Hatfield District Council for permission to create a major new shopping area and railway travel centre which would entail the demolition of the ticket hall. It was hoped that this plan might revitalise the town centre, then rapidly losing its specialist shops. In the meantime planning consent was given to Park Plaza, a shopping/leisure complex above the A1M Motorway tunnel at Hatfield and this cast doubt as to whether the Welwyn Garden City scheme would proceed. At the time of writing (May 1986) it seems likely that the development will go ahead.

In LNER days, on the main line at Welwyn, Post Office mail bag apparatus was sited 20¼ yards south of Digswell signal box at the south end of the viaduct near Digswell Junction. It was used to collect mail bags by two week-night mail trains leaving Kings Cross at 8.25 pm and 10.35 pm.

2.5 The branch lines

Originally Hatfield was the principal junction, where main line trains connected with branch services to St Albans, Hertford and Luton and Dunstable, as did the local services from Kings Cross, Moorgate and Broad Street which terminated at Hatfield.

Both the Luton–Dunstable and Hertford branches passed through attractive countryside after leaving Welwyn Garden City. On the former, the line turned sharply westward and to

Figure 2.8   *The new Welwyn Garden City station officially opened on 5 October 1926*
                                                                      © *British Railways*

Figure 2.9   *Welwyn Garden City station showing the up and (left) the Hertford branch platforms on the last day of passenger services on the branch line, 16 June 1951. Class N7 0–6–2T No 69695 heads the 6.51 pm departure for Hertford North. Note the east side booking office (since removed) attached to the footbridge*
Courtesy of Real Photographs

the rear of the Cherry Tree public house and the Campus complex, under Digswell Road (the White Bridge), up a steep gradient through Sherrards Park and Brock's Woods and under the old Great North Road at Digswell Hill. This section, although overgrown since it was closed to freight traffic in 1970,

can still be traced most of the way to the site of Ayot station. For the next 2½ miles the track bed becomes part of the Ayot Greenway, a public nature walk prepared and managed by the Countryside Management Service on behalf of the Hertfordshire County Council. Thence the line followed the Lea valley through Wheathampstead, Chiltern Green and on to Luton and Dunstable.

The Hertford branch continued northward after leaving the east side of Welwyn Garden City station and then, immediately beyond the buffer stops of what is now a siding, diverged south east through what became the north-eastern industrial area and across Bessemer Road and Tewin Road. The overbridge in Tewin Road was demolished in 1986. Continuing south-east the line passed close to Attimore Hall where there was a Halt (closed 1 July 1905) and continued in this direction, crossing Cole Green Lane on the level just short of its junction with Black Fan Road. The track bed is still visible looking back from this former road crossing. The line then continued through what is now the Cole Green rubbish tip (to which trains conveyed refuse until 1966) to cross the main A414 Hatfield to Hertford road by an underbridge, since demolished in connection with road improvements. The line was finally closed on 23 May 1966. From the A414 road the track passed through Cole Green and Hertingfordbury to the railway viaduct at Hertford. Like the Luton branch it has been made into a public nature walk, known as Cole Green Way, by the Hertfordshire County Council.

The third branch line based on Hatfield was the six-mile single line to St Albans, the route of which is still visible, which diverged westward immediately north of Hatfield station and passed through unexciting countryside to its destination at the London & North Western Railway's St Albans Abbey station. It was opened on 16 October 1865. The track bed is also still visible at a number of places and the station platform and building at Smallford are still extant and occupied by a scrap metal merchant. This branch never developed as an east–west route as envisaged and was closed to passenger traffic on 1

October 1951. The position of Welwyn and the branch lines referred to in relation to the railway network at its peak is shown in Figure 1.1.

2.6 Amalgamation and nationalisation

Under the Railways Act 1921, the Great Northern Railway became part of the London & North Eastern Railway on 1 January 1923. Later under the Transport Act 1947, the major railways of Great Britain were nationalised to become British Railways under the overall control of the British Transport Commission. On 1 January 1948, the Great Northern East Coast Main Line became part of British Railways Eastern Region.

Figure 2.10   The goods shed at Welwyn Garden City, demolished in May 1986
Courtesy of Welwyn Garden City Library

Chapter 3

Welwyn North

As built for the commencement of passenger, goods and coal traffic in 1850, Welwyn station was a typical rural example of the period. It appears to have remained substantially unchanged until partial modernisation in 1966–7, and the removal of the remaining goods and coal facilities in December 1970.

The principal buildings were situated on the up side and comprised the station master's house, booking office, waiting rooms including – even in 1986 – a ladies' waiting room, staff rooms and toilets. The whole was built with slated roofs and red bricks which were made locally and are unique to railway buildings at Welwyn. The original waiting room on the down platform was built of timber. (*See* Figure 2.4)

In a stretch of railway only 3450 feet long, between the north end of Digswell Viaduct and the south portal of Welwyn South Tunnel, existed a complex system of sidings and crossovers. These were provided to meet the needs of the mainly agricultural community which was to be served by Welwyn station. At the time of construction the nearest stations were at Hatfield 4¼ miles to the south and Stevenage 6½ miles to the north. The present Stevenage station is on a new site, only 5½ miles to the north; that is, one mile further south. The nearest stations in 1986 are Knebworth, opened in 1884, and Welwyn Garden City, opened in 1926.

The up platform was originally about 415 feet long, terminating at its north end at the driveway from Harmer Green Lane, which is extant in 1986 and still used to gain access to the line for maintenance purposes. This driveway led to a loading bay and cattle dock served by two sidings to the east of the up line and extending to the tunnel mouth. (*See* Figure

Figure 3.1 *Diagram of Welwyn station in 1907, based on an official GNR drawing. Key to plan: 1 station building, 2 Cowper Arms Hotel, 3 signal box, 4 goods shed, 5 five-ton crane, 6 weighbridge, 7 stables, 8 carriage dock 9 platforms*

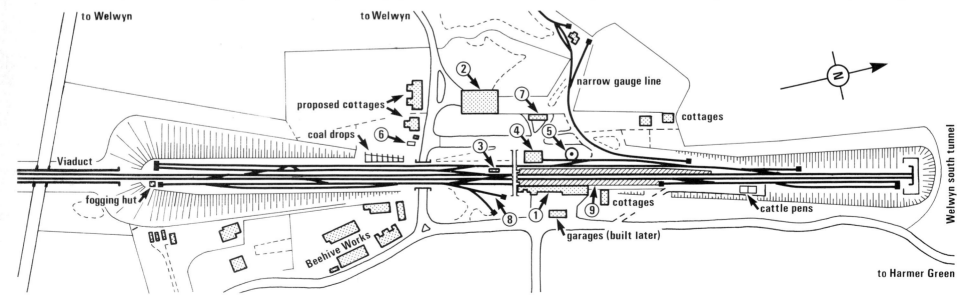

3.5.) At some time after 17 November 1935, when the signals and points connecting to the up main line were disconnected, these sidings and pens were removed and the platform was extended to its present length of about 610 feet. Access to the sidings was by reversal from the up main line. At the south end of the up platform there were three short sidings where horses and carriages could be loaded from a ramp onto special vehicles. An attractive red-brick retaining wall with stone dressings, revealing the slope of the ramp, may still be seen adjacent to Harmer Green Lane. These sidings later became a coal yard and the area is now used for storing contractor's plant. Access to these sidings was also by reversal from the up line. Close to this point was a trailing crossover from the up to the down main line. There were other sidings to the south which passed behind the Beehive Works to terminate at buffer stops at the viaduct.

Facilities on the down side were more extensive. Two coal sidings with a coal drop were provided between the viaduct and the Station Road underbridge. The coal yard and original coal drops are still in existence in 1986 though no longer served by rail. These are the last intact original coal drops on the GN line, those at Kings Cross having been partially demolished despite being listed buildings. North of the underbridge the sidings extended alongside the signal box (demolished 1973), under the footbridge and through a substantial brick built and slate-roofed goods shed. Just south of the footbridge a wagon turntable and spur gave access to a timber yard on the site of the October 1984 extension to the car park. North of the goods shed a second siding to the west gave access to a loading bay equipped with a crane and a cattle pen. The two sidings merged to form a junction with the down main line opposite the north end of the up platform. This junction was later moved further north with the first lengthening of the down platform. This platform was extended for a second time immediately prior to electrification, to its present length of 610 feet.

In its heyday, as can be envisaged from the 1898 and 1907 plans (*see* Figures. 2.1 and 3.1), the scene at Welwyn station

must have been a very busy one as all classes of traffic appear to have been catered for. On arrival the goods trains were shunted into position by their locomotives. However, until well after 1945, internal shunting was, to a large degree, carried out by horse. The last horse was a well-known character by the name of Tom whose photograph appeared in the *London and North Eastern Railway Magazine*. (*See* Figure 9.3.) The horses were housed in a purpose-built brick stable which still exists in 1986 (*see* Figure 3.7), being leased to a scrap plastic recovery firm. Unfortunately the building has lost its characteristic GNR clerestory-type roof. A nearby forage store was demolished in October 1984 to make way for the car park extension. Well after

Figure 3.2   Welwyn station c.1900 showing the mid-morning departure for Peterborough hauled by a GNR Stirling 4–2–2 as rebuilt with a domed boiler. Note the sidings and cattle dock nearing completion.   Courtesy of Real Photographs Co.

the Second World War ended, deliveries of goods were effected by horse and cart – another duty for Tom, until the arrival of a Karrier Kob motor vehicle and trailer.

A pair of brick and slated cottages for railway employees was built facing the forecourt on the east side of the station. Another pair and a single cottage were built above the sidings on the west side. All these cottages still exist in 1986. A proposal to build further cottages for employees in Station Road opposite the Cowper Arms never materialised. A footbridge spanning the main lines and west side sidings gave access to the up and down platforms. This bridge (*see* Chapter 4) does not appear in

Figure 3.3   GNR Class C1 'Atlantic' No 250 hauling an up stopping morning train from Peterborough c.1907. Note the horse-drawn skips on the narrow gauge railway
© *Photomatic Ltd*

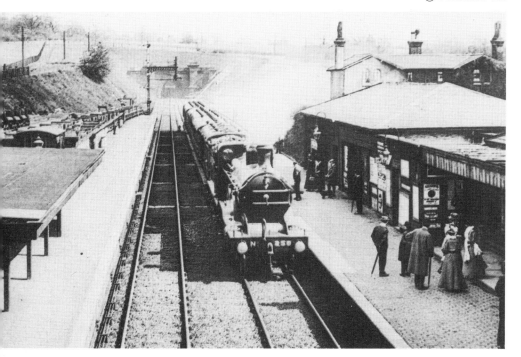

early photographs (*see* Figure 2.3) and its date of construction is uncertain. Although shortened after the down sidings were removed it continues to serve as a useful station entrance for passengers approaching from the west side.

Earlier facilities at the station included a GPO letter box, a GPO telephone kiosk and a newspaper stall on the up platform. The last of these to go was the telephone kiosk which was resited on the corner of Adele Avenue on 15 December 1964, but it was relocated on the station forecourt on 22 August 1986.

After 1945 goods traffic quickly went into decline and bulk coal deliveries for the Welwyn area concentrated on a depot at Garston, near Watford, in late 1962. All goods facilities were withdrawn from the station during 1966 and 1967. The station was closed to livestock traffic in about 1980, although none had actually been handled for some time, and to parcels traffic soon after. Left luggage facilities were withdrawn in 1977. Apart from bicycles few items were latterly deposited, the last being a tuba in 1976.

A partial modernisation of the station took place at the end of 1964 when the footbridge was reduced in length and the old down side (northbound) waiting room replaced by a small modern shelter. After deducting the width forward of the yellow line marking the limit of the safe standing area when InterCity 125 High Speed Trains are passing, this shelter reduces the effective platform width to two feet. The goods shed, then one of the few nesting sites of the Black Redstart in Hertfordshire, was demolished and the sidings were removed soon afterwards. Older buildings on the up platform were substantially rebuilt to provide the gentlemen's toilet, station-master's office – now used as a store – and general waiting room. Perhaps the most important work was the heightening of the platforms in readiness for the new electric train services. The steps from the booking hall, which is at the original plat-form level, to the present platform, and from the latter down to the covered sitting area north of the ladies waiting room are the results of this work and have proved a hazard to the unwary.

In the mid 1960s lock-up garages on the up side forecourt were demolished to increase car parking space. In connection with this development the organisers of the Digswell entry in the Best Kept Village Competition negotiated with British Railways for a rose bed to be contained within a brick trough spanning the frontage of the station to Harmer Green Lane. Part of the deal was that British Railways would provide a truck load of soil to fill the trough, free of charge, and the Digswell Horticultural Society would purchase and plant some forty Elizabeth of Glamis roses. These were duly planted and remained a feature until 1983 when the Society replaced the roses with Hypericum.

Until September 1973 movements of trains through Welwyn North were controlled from the signal box, which was situated adjacent to the south end of the down platform. Due to physical conditions, the signalling system between Welwyn Garden City and Woolmer Green was a complex one. The Welwyn North box was responsible for all signal and points movements between the south end of the viaduct and the approach to Woolmer Green. The box was closed on 16 September 1973,

Figure 3.4   *View from the footbridge at Welwyn station, looking south, 13 May 1908. Note the tall signal post (Welwyn down home 23) and the Welwyn starter signal affixed to the third arch of the viaduct*
By courtesy of the National Railway Museum, York

and demolished during the following December when colour light signals were installed in connection with a scheme, brought fully into operation in April 1977, for controlling all train movements from a new power signal box at York Road, Kings Cross, which had opened on 26 September 1971. (*See* Chapter 5.)

At the time of the station improvements in 1964 the former British Railways, Eastern Region, blue totem station name signs were replaced by black and white signs of the present design and fluorescent lighting on reinforced concrete posts was installed. In 1982 the original fluorescent lights were replaced by a new design on steel posts and the name signs removed. The new lights had the station name applied to the diffusers. In 1985 high-intensity sodium lights, complying with illumination

requirements for driver-only trains, and new black and white station signs were fitted to the existing steel posts. The posts were repainted red in 1986 for the launching of the 'Network SouthEast' campaign on 10 June.

With driver-only operation it is interesting to note that no mirrors giving the driver a view of the train and platform to the rear have been installed at Welwyn North, presumably because the track is straight here.

A further phase of modernisation was carried out in June 1984, when an additional section of land on the west side of the station was surfaced to provide further car parking space. On 18 October 1984 work began on a yet more ambitious scheme on the west side to provide a total of 170 parking spaces at a cost of £17 000. This it was hoped would discourage kerb-side parking in Harmer Green Lane and Adele Avenue on the east side of the station, and parking restrictions were imposed there from 7 July 1985. Charges for parking at the station were reduced in April 1985 from £85 to £65 per year.

In September 1985 the station advertisement hoardings were repainted and in the following month they were removed and replaced by weatherproof lockable notice boards. Flower baskets were supplied to Welwyn North and many other stations during the summer of 1985; those at Welwyn North have been especially well tended despite occasional damage by vandals and weather.

In February 1986 many years' accumulation of undergrowth was cleared from the southbound platform to allow the station garden to be restored. It is to be maintained by the Digswell Women's Institute under an agreement between British Rail and the National Federation of Women's Institutes whereby British Rail will meet half the cost of establishing amenity areas and facilities.

In April 1986 at a parish meeting in Welwyn 60 per cent of

Figure 3.5   *View from the north end of Welwyn station showing the cattle dock and sidings in use*

Plate 3   *Welwyn North station at night on 8 February 1986*

© *T. W. Gladwin*

those present voted against a proposal to change the station name to Digswell.

It is fortunate that despite the changes described Welwyn North station building is basically unaltered since its construction in 1850 and is now one of the few original surviving examples on the GN Main Line. In view of this, representations have been made for the station, including the footbridge and unique coal drop, to be scheduled as a Listed Building, for both special architectural and historic reasons. (*See* Plate 5.)

Figure 3.6   *A pre-1928 morning stopping train to Peterborough at Welwyn station hauled by LNER Class A1 'Pacific' No 4474* Victor Wild. *Note the GNR somersault signals and junction to the cattle sidings on the right*   © *J. A. Coltas*

Figure 3.7   *The former shunting horse stable at Welwyn North station now used for industrial purposes, 17 March 1986*   © *T. W. Gladwin*

Meanwhile, to the aesthetic distaste of some, electric catenary was erected across the viaduct and on through the station in 1974–6 in connection with the Kings Cross to Royston electric services which commenced on 6 February 1978. For the record, the first passenger-carrying electric train to call at Welwyn North was a special train, comprising unit No 313 029 of the inner suburban stock, to Kings Cross, carrying passengers who wished to see the celebrations on the occasion of the Queen's Silver Jubilee on 7 June 1977. The train carried a special commemorative headboard. (*See* Figure 3.9.)

A photograph of the station taken in 1907 (*see* Figure 3.3) or thereabouts shows a row of contractor's skips on narrow gauge rails to the immediate west of the down side sidings. Enquiries have revealed that this contractor's light railway was laid from Lockleys, then the home of George Dering and now part of Sherrardswood School, to the station, and was to enable surplus spoil from the diversion of the Hertford–Welwyn Road (from the front of Lockleys to its present route) to be taken away by rail. This diversion was completed in 1907 at the expense of 'Squire' Dering. Photographs in the Welwyn Hatfield Museum show the work in progress in Hertford Road, with wagons being hauled by a narrow gauge steam 0-4-0 saddle tank. The station photograph, however, shows the skips being hauled by a white horse. The route followed by this line is shown on the plan of Welwyn station dated November 1907 (*see* Figure 3.1). From the down side goods yard it crossed Cob Lane Common along what is now the path from the car park to the north end of Woodside Road.

Such was the impression given to passengers travelling north from Kings Cross as they passed through tunnel after tunnel, nine to Woolmer Green, that in 1910 E. M. Forster, in his book *Howards End*, referred to a journey by Mrs Munt to Howards End, a house at Hilton, as follows:

> The train sped northward, under innumerable tunnels. It was only an hour's journey, but Mrs Munt had to raise and lower the window again and again. She passed through the South Welwyn Tunnel and saw light for a moment and entered North Welwyn Tunnel, of tragic fame. She traversed the immense viaduct whose arches span untroubled meadows and the dreamy flow of Tewin Water. She skirted the parks of politicians. At times the Great North Road accompanied her, more suggestive of infinity than any railway, awakening, after a nap of a hundred years, to such life as is conferred by the stench of motor cars, and to such culture as is implied by the advertisements of anti-bilious pills.

The station for Hilton was, of course, Knebworth.

As an indication of the amount of traffic handled by the railway in more active times, Bob Cutts recalls the days between 1936 and 1939 when he was employed as Outward Clerk at Welwyn North as well as Inward Clerk at Knebworth. During this period the station staff numbered fifteen, the station being manned every day from the arrival of the first train to the departure of the last. The staff consisted of the Stationmaster, Chief Goods Clerk, Inward and Outward Clerks, two Booking

Clerks, Leading Porter, two other porters and a lad, drayman/shunt horse driver, motor vehicle driver and three signalmen. In addition there were permanent-way staff and of course the shunt horse, Tom. The staff now consists of one booking clerk who works 0645–1421 hours [*sic*], Mondays to Fridays. The establishment also makes provision for two leading railmen alternately working 0630–1430 and 1430–2230.

Bob Cutts recalls joining the LNER on leaving school and, after training at stations between Welwyn Garden City and the old Stevenage, was posted to Welwyn North in 1936 at the age of 18. His daily duties commenced at Knebworth where he would clear the invoices which had accumulated from the

Figure 3.8   *Welwyn North station in 1963 prior to alterations. Note the telephone kiosk on the up platform. The railway employee is Ken Risborough*   © *Photomatic Ltd*

Plate 4 *BR Class 312 electric multiple unit (EMU) No 312/704 approaching the up platform at Welwyn North station, 15 July 1985* © *W. Clark*

previous morning before catching a mid-morning train to Welwyn North, sometimes passing messages to Woolmer Green signal box *en route* by throwing them, weighted by a piece of track ballast, from the train as it passed! Once at Welwyn North he would have speedily dealt with the invoices here in preparation for the down pick-up goods train, No. 317, at 11.35 am. The invoices referred to had to be put behind spring clips on the wagon sides. The next duty would be to prepare the invoices for the 'London Motor' which was an experimental road service for parcels, arriving from Marylebone in the morning and returning in the early afternoon. The invoices were stamped

'Motor to London' and routed by Marylebone and Quainton Road. The motor was usually an old Thorneycroft 1920-vintage vehicle, modernised with pneumatic tyres, electric lights and a windscreen. The driver's uniform included leather gaiters!

His duties also included the charging of demurrage for wagons which overstayed their unloading time before being returned empty. To improve his knowledge of railway work,

Figure 3.9   *The first passenger-carrying electric train to call at Welwyn North station, 'The Silver Jubilee Special' on 7 June 1977, with Class 313 electric multiple unit No 029 leading the six-coach train*   © *G. W. Goslin*

Bob attended evening classes. first at Marylebone on 'Goods Station Work and Accounts' and then at Liverpool Street on 'Block Signalling'. As there was no convenient train to London he used to walk across the viaduct to join a train at Welwyn Garden City – a highly irregular and dangerous practice! During his viaduct walks he was particularly impressed by the sensation of hammer-like blows by passing locomotives on the structure.

Life at Welwyn North during this period (1936–9) seems to have been pleasant and friendly, but not without its serious moments. Bob recalls an occasion when a down Leeds express ran through adverse signals. As it crossed the viaduct it was

Figure 3.10 *Welwyn North station as partially modernised in the 1960s. Note the up High Speed Train was in yellow and blue livery* © W. Clark

rapidly catching up with the down all stations 'Parly', an Atlantic locomotive hauling eight coaches. The signalman, Horace Ball, leapt from his box and managed to place two detonators on the line in front of the Pacific-hauled Leeds train. This alerted the driver, who was able to slow down his train and an accident was averted. Horace Ball was commended for his swift action and later remote controlled detonators were fitted and operated from the signal box.

Another episode Bob recounts resulted from the fact that at the time when he was attending evening classes on block signalling, he was allowed in the signal box to gain practical experience. On one such occasion Horace Ball was busy entering his logbook when one beat on the bell came through from Welwyn Garden City box. 'Take that one' Horace said to Bob. So Bob acknowledged the single bell and received the four bell code (express train) for the 'Queen of Scots Pullman' from Welwyn Garden City which he duly passed forward to Woolmer Green box. All was well, so he thought, until he heard a long crow on the whistle from the approaching train indicating that he had not pulled the 'home' signal off. By then the Pullman was at a crawling pace and passed Welwyn North box with the guard staring out of his window in surprise at this unusual delay! Subsequently the usual 'please explain' routine was instituted but Horace Ball took it all in good part – as it was actually his responsibility.

Less dramatic but more frequent were the fire brigade call-outs. The staff attached to the two coal merchants at Welwyn North – Burgess and Payne – were volunteer members of the Welwyn Fire Brigade and whenever the maroon was fired there would be a mad rush to clamber on to Payne's green lorry for the 1½ mile trip to Welwyn to join the fire engine.

Such were the earlier days at Welwyn North! Expresses continue to roar through as always, but freight trains are substantially fewer. Happily the outer suburban trains call at regular intervals and there is still a cheery greeting from the station staff.

Chapter 4

Viaducts, Bridges and Tunnels

4.1 Viaducts

The greatest obstacle to overcome during the construction of the Great Northern Railway between London and Peterborough was undoubtedly the crossing of the Mimram valley. The route chosen, as surveyed by William Cubitt, required a means of crossing this valley and hence Welwyn Viaduct, also regularly referred to as Digswell Viaduct, was planned and built. Designed by Lewis Cubitt, and constructed by the contractor Thomas Brassey, it cost £69 397.

Comprising forty 30ft-span arches, reaching up to 98 feet above the river, Welwyn Viaduct is stated by Grinling (rev. ed. 1966) to be 1490 feet long. Elsewhere the Department of the

Figure 4.1 *Newly constructed Welwyn viaduct, from a lithograph in the* Illustrated London News, *10 August 1850*   © *Illustrated London News*

Environment, in their *List of Buildings of Special Architectural or Historic Interest*, give the length as 1545 feet and, as a result of a typographical error, incorrectly state that it has 49 arches. However, the original plans reproduced in the *Record of Modern Engineering* (1864) show the length to be 1563 feet (521 yards) and British Railways (personal communication) say it is 1557 feet (519 yards). Thus Cockman (1983) and Gladwin, Neville and White (1985) give the length as *about* 1560 feet. The overall height was increased in the autumn of 1974 by the addition of metal gantries to carry overhead electric wires.

For the construction of the viaduct, brick earth was available close to the site and the contractor opened up two brickfields on the sides of the valley. One was to the north of St John's Church, Digswell and the other adjacent to Digswell Lodge. The *Welwyn Times* (23 March 1984) quotes the late William Horn as seeing the bricks used in the building of the viaduct being made on a site near the present Stonehills. As William Horn was not born until some twenty-one years after the viaduct was completed, it seems possible this reference is to one of the later brickworks, possibly that on the lower Handside Farm west of Sherrards Wood School, used in the development of Welwyn Garden City. (*See* Chapter 2.) The viaduct as originally completed required five million bricks.

Robert (1962) records that the foundations for the viaduct were formed by digging 'an enormous trench 2,000 feet long, 300 feet wide, and 100 feet deep' and packing the excavation so formed with 'loads of burnt clay and mortar' to provide a firm and indestructible base. Such a trench would have involved the removal of over 2.2 million cubic yards of material. Early accounts (*Record of Modern Engineering*, 1864) and plans gave the excavations for the foundations as 17 957 cubic yards and describe the construction as follows:

> It is built of kiln-burnt bricks, the whole, excepting the abutments, being carried up in cement. In consequence of the peculiar nature of the ground in the lower part of the valley, 11 piers [*numbers 7 to 17 inclusive from the south end*] were timbered. The foundation of each of these is formed by 65 piers, 12 inches square, which were driven by a steam pile engine with an 18 cwt monkey, until they would not sink 1/8 inch with a blow of 20 feet fall. They were then cross braced and planked as shown by drawings.

Figure 4.2   *Welwyn (or Digswell) viaduct approach embankment under construction in 1850, detail from a pastel and charcoal sketch by Samuel Lucas*
Courtesy of Hitchin Museum

The novelty in the construction consists in the piers and abutments being cellular, bonded at intervals with Yorkshire paving, having four courses of brickwork on each bond. The arches are turned with four rings throughout its extra thickness for increase of strength being four additional rings, forming back ribs, bonded to the main arch as shown on enlarged section. [*sic*]

[See folded plan inside back cover]

The piers batter 1 in 30 on the ends and 1 in 40 on the sides. The imposts, string course, and coping are of Warden stone. The quantities are as follows:

Timber in 11 foundations	19,844 cubic feet
Wrought iron in pile shoes and bond	26,387 lbs
Excavation in foundations	17,957 cubic yards
Brickwork in mortar	4,485 cubic yards
Brickwork in cement	31,338 cubic yards
Masonry	45,662 cubic feet
6 inch iron water pipe	1,874 feet

Cost £69,397 or £133.4s per lineal yard.

For comparison, the average cost of the whole line from London to York was about £13 per yard of route.

As is not uncommon in engineering, delays occurred during construction of the viaduct, mainly due to exceptionally hard frosts bringing work to a halt during the winter prior to the planned opening day. Even so, construction took only two years – no mean feat when it is remembered that there were no mechanical aids and only horses for the transport of the materials. It is said that five to six thousand navvies were employed on the whole project from London to Peterborough.

The original pastel and charcoal sketch by Samuel Lucas of 'Digswell Viaduct' under construction which hangs in the Hitchin Museum is reproduced in Foster (1981). (*See* Figure 4.2). The newly completed viaduct was also the subject of a fine lithograph which appeared in the *Illustrated London News* of 10 August 1850. (*See* Figure 4.1).

It was reported in January 1858 that longitudinal cracks had appeared in the brickwork of the arches of the viaduct. The engineer said drivers of up coal trains were crossing at speeds in excess of 40 mph. Tie rods were inserted to arrest the cracks and a 15 mph speed restriction imposed on goods and mineral trains.

The viaduct was originally faced with red bricks which proved to be too porous. This is evident from photographs showing white lines of salts that had been leached out of the structure. (*See* Figure 4.3). Thus an outer skin of harder blue facing bricks was added. This work was completed in October 1935 at a cost of £25 000. It had taken fourteen men five years and required 1 181 000 blue bricks, 1100 tons of sand and 650 tons of cement. About 1965 tie bars were added to reinforce the bond between the two skins of brickwork. Copies of a superb painting of the viaduct by S. R. Badmin, showing the original fine red bricks, adorned carriage compartments on the line for many years. Part of the original red brick facade is still visible at the south end of the viaduct and is best viewed from Bessemer Road.

As the viaduct is a Grade II Listed Building, British Railways require planning permission for even small changes. In June 1984, application was made to Welwyn Hatfield District Council to fit a plastic drain pipe on each side of every fourth pier to drain away rainwater which had percolated through the track bed. The application, No C6/362/84LB, included very useful plans of the viaduct. The works concerned were started in late 1984 but were delayed when several tons of the contractor's scaffolding, already erected around one pier, were stolen during one weekend. On 18 May 1986 British Rail started work to waterproof the track bed of the viaduct with a rubberised material. This operation was expected to last 12–14 weekends and included the task of fitting the black plastic drainpipes deferred from 1984.

The first train to cross the viaduct was a 'special' which left Maiden Lane for Peterborough on Monday 5 August 1850. Queen Victoria soon made a rail journey on the Great Northern line. She left London (Maiden Lane) at 2 pm on 27 August 1851, to travel to Balmoral via Boston, Lincoln and Doncaster, breaking her journey at Doncaster where she stayed overnight at the Angel Hotel. It is recorded that she requested the train to be stopped at the south end of Welwyn Viaduct so that she could alight and cross the valley on foot, to rejoin the train at Welwyn station – a most unlikely story!

It is interesting to note that the viaduct originally carried only fourteen weekday passenger trains and a few goods and coal trains, compared with approximately 280 trains a day in 1986.

Apart from the refacing work already referred to, the viaduct has withstood the test of time. At the time of its construction locomotives, carriages and wagons were light in weight but over the years they have gradually become heavier and faster. The high speed steam-hauled trains of the immediate pre- and post-war period must have been a constant source of apprehension to the Chief Civil Engineer of the day. So far as the authors

Figure 4.3 *Welwyn viaduct in 1908 showing the salt markings on the brickwork*
By courtesy of the National Railway Museum, York

Figure 4.4 *The viaduct as seen from the Hertford Road, looking west in 1915*
© *Hertfordshire County Library*

are aware, the only weight restriction placed on the viaduct was that Pacific (4-6-2) locomotives were not to be used in pairs over the viaduct. As for today, the speed restriction over the viaduct and through the station is 115 mph, reducing to 105 mph through the two Welwyn tunnels.

A second smaller viaduct of 198 feet in length crosses Robbery Bottom Lane at Oaklands, a quarter mile north of Welwyn North Tunnel. Properly known as Robbery Wood Viaduct, it consists of seven arches of 22 feet span, is 27 feet 8 inches between the parapets, and is 56 feet from the road, Robbery Bottom Lane, to the level of the rails. The piers and abutments are of solid brickwork. The bricks were kiln burnt and the mortar was composed of stone, lime and sand. The imposts, string course and coping are of dressed Portland stone (*Record of Modern Engineering*, 1864). The quantities in this viaduct are given as follows:

Excavating for foundations	900 cubic yards
Brickwork in piers, abutments and parapets, mortar	2,497 cubic yards
Brickwork in arches, spandrils &c, in cement	656 cubic yards
Portland stone in imposts; string course, and coping	2,096 cubic feet

Cost £4,643 or £70 7s per lineal yard.

4.2   Bridges

Ten overbridges were constructed across the main line between Welwyn Garden City and Woolmer Green of which nine remain. The most southerly of the bridges, Sandpit Bridge (formerly Tommy Dell's Bridge) demolished in 1974, was used to convey materials on a narrow gauge railway (*see* Chapter 2) from the sandpits and brickworks on the east side of the main line to sites under development in Welwyn Garden City in the 1920s.

Twentieth Mile Bridge which, as its name suggests, is situated twenty miles from Kings Cross, carries Stanborough Road over the line. It also provides a fine view of the flyover immediately south of Welwyn Garden City station. This was constructed in 1973–5 to allow inner suburban electric multiple units to move between the down side sidings north of the station, the down platforms, and the up lines and platforms without disrupting main line and outer suburban services.

A footbridge erected when Welwyn Garden City station was built in 1926 leads from the booking hall on the west side to both of the double-faced platforms. As was noted in Chapter 2, this footbridge was extended in 1936 to provide both an access to the station and a walkway to the town centre from the east side of the line. (*See* Figure 2.9.)

Immediately north of Welwyn Garden City station is Hunters Bridge which carries Bridge Road (formerly Hunters Lane) over the main line. Built about 1868 it provided access to Pear Tree

Farm tenanted by the Hunter family whose name it bears. By 1919 this bridge was said to be 'in very poor condition' and when the LNER failed to satisfy its liability to maintain the structure the District Council repaired and widened it in 1929–30. It was further repaired and expanded in 1960 when the dual carriageways were provided.

Lyle's Bridge, named after William Lyle of Digswell Lodge and Digswell Water farms, is located half a mile north of Welwyn Garden City station. Originally built by the railway for access to Digswell Lodge Farm it connects Digswell Rise and Lyles Lane, now a cycle track which leads into the rear of the former ICI premises. At the time of writing (May 1986) proposals for its demolition are under consideration.

Some 350 yards further north a modern bridge, finally completed in 1960, carries Knightsfield over the line and provides the principal road link between the Haldens and central areas of Welwyn Garden City.

Figure 4.5   *The pre-war down 'Flying Scotsman' crossing the viaduct behind LNER Class A3 'Pacific' No 2746* Fairway   *Courtesy of D. E. White*

The next overbridge is the footbridge linking the platforms at Welwyn North. This fine bridge is one of the few remaining examples of the earliest GNR footbridges although its precise date of construction is uncertain. Originally there were no foot-bridges on the GNR, most platforms being connected by wooden crossings laid between the running lines or, in a few cases, by subways. This explains the absence of the bridge in the earliest pictures of Welwyn station which do however show a wooden crossing between the south ends of the platforms. This crossing continued to be maintained and used by railway staff until removal in 1978.

Two road bridges cross the line at Woolmer Green. The more southerly comprises three arches and carries the former Great North Road, there known as Mardley Hill. Almost adjacent is a bridge carrying Heath Road over the line.

Although it is just beyond the section of the GNR principally considered in this book, it is worth noting that the railway bridge immediately north of Knebworth station, sometimes known as Big Span Bridge, is the largest brick span between London and York.

4.3 Tunnels

The first 23½ miles of the main line from Kings Cross to Woolmer Green pass through no fewer than nine tunnels with a total length of some 5756 yards (3¼ miles) which encase 14 per cent of this stretch of line. The tunnels vary in length between 1214 yards (Potters Bar) and 232 yards (Hadley North). As mentioned in Chapter 2, all the tunnels are straight as the techniques for constructing curved tunnels were still, in 1850, considered inadequate.

Two tunnels, complete with visible smoke vents, pass through the chalk at Welwyn. Welwyn South Tunnel, formerly Lockleys Hill Tunnel, which proudly bears the date of its construction (1850) on its south portal, is 447 yards long. Welwyn North Tunnel, shown on early maps as Harmer Green

Figure 4.6   *The tunnels at Welwyn viewed from the up platform of Welwyn North station, 15 July 1985*   © *T. W. Gladwin*

Tunnel, is much longer at 1047 yards. At some time the tunnels must have been officially remeasured as the *GNR Appendix for 1912* and earlier GNR publications quote the lengths as 446 and 1046 yards respectively.

A major accident which occurred in Welwyn North Tunnel on 9 June 1866 is described in Chapter 12.

At the time of writing (1986) the banks of the cuttings between the two tunnels and between Welwyn South Tunnel and Welwyn North station are among the richest wildlife sites in and around Digswell village. However the rich chalk flowers such as orchids, and locally scarce animals such as lizards, grass snakes and slow worms, are threatened by the recent rapid scrub invasion. Such undesirable colonisation was originally controlled by planned and, in the days of steam hauled trains, accidental burning.

The viaducts, bridges, tunnels and other structures such as the station buildings continue to suffer continual heavy vibration but remain open. Such was the vision and quality of engineering of the railway pioneers during the 1840s and 1850s.

Chapter 5

Signals and Signalling

Until the advent of centrally controlled colour lights, the generally accepted system of signalling on British Railways was that of the block section. Under this system the whole railway was divided into sections, each under the total and separate control of a single dedicated signal box. The lengths of the sections varied but were largely determined by the density of traffic and the number and use of junctions, sidings and other facilities.

The principle of block working is that no two trains should be allowed into any one section at the same time. Thus the signals governing the exit from a block section are returned to the danger, i.e. on, position after each train has passed. This protects the first train by not allowing a following train to enter the section it occupies. Further protection was provided by the later addition of a system known as electrical track circuiting. Under this system a small voltage is applied across the rails. A train, or obstruction across the rails, is detected when it completes the circuit and so causes a flow of electrical current. It is wired up to prevent a signalman from accepting a train from the preceding signal box by locking his entry into section signal in the on position until his own section is clear. Regulations do however permit more than one train in a section for specified purposes such as shunting, or in the event of a breakdown or accident. A still safer system known as The Welwyn Control, is referred to in Chapter 12 in relation to the 1935 accident at Welwyn Garden City.

Although not all were always provided, the normal order in which a train driver would approach the signals for each block section would be:

(1) *Outer Distant Signal* which gives the driver early notice of the position of the *Home* and *Starting signals*. A *distant* signal is not a stop signal and may therefore be passed when in the caution position.

(2) *Inner Distant Signal* which also indicates the position of the *Home signal*.

(3) *Home Signal* which is normally situated so that a train driver sees it just before reaching a station

(4) *Starting Signal* which is usually located at or just beyond the front end of a platform

(5) *Advanced Starting Signal* which is located beyond the starter so that when required it can be used to control the forward movements of trains coming from sidings and other lines situated beyond the *Starting signal*.

The Great Northern main line was originally constructed having up (to London) and down (from London) running lines with lay-by sidings at intervals. These latter were gradually joined up to provide additional running lines and much time was saved once the slow running goods trains had their own tracks. By this means four tracks became available at the south end of Digswell Viaduct (Digswell Junction) and between Woolmer Green and Knebworth in 1877, leaving only two tracks between Digswell Junction and Woolmer Green. The three signal boxes immediately responsible for this section were at Digswell, Welwyn (later Welwyn North), and Woolmer Green.

The stretch of line between what is now Welwyn Garden City and Woolmer Green was a complex one requiring special treatment. There is a rising gradient of 1 in 200 from Welwyn Garden City to the south end of the viaduct after which comes Welwyn North station which, until the 1960s, had three separate sets of sidings, followed by Welwyn South and North tunnels. These features collectively created great difficulties in siting signals to the adequate vantage of the drivers. Thus, in earlier days, particularly when the line was part of the GNR, there were some unusually tall signal posts (*see* Figure 3.4) and

Figure 5.1 *Lineside indicator for Digswell Junction at the south end of Welwyn viaduct, February 1986* © *T. W. Gladwin*

other special arrangements. For example, there has never been a starting signal at the front end of the up platform at Welwyn North.

Since 1911 the signalling system in the Welwyn area has been variously altered to accommodate changes in traffic conditions and speeds, recommendations following accidents, the growth of Welwyn Garden City, and various technical developments. The most recent and indeed most radical alterations took place in the 1960s and 1970s. These followed the withdrawal of the loose coupled goods, mineral trains and local goods trains and consequential closure of local sidings, together with the general increase in speeds of both express and local trains. At this time the entire signalling system was replaced by colour-light multiple-aspect signals controlled, together with points, from a new central control situated at Kings Cross (York Road). As a result of this all signal boxes between Kings Cross and Sandy and Royston became redundant and most have been demolished.

The functions of the signal boxes at Digswell, Welwyn North, and Woolmer Green are described in the sections that follow. The numbers in parentheses () refer to the signal lever numbers in the box responsible for those signals. Reference to Figures 5.2 , 5.4 and 5.10 will assist in identifying the signals described and the box from which they were operated.

5.1 Digswell signal box

This signal box was situated on the down side of the line between the end of the four track system and the south end of the viaduct. The down goods line was extended to this point in 1895 and the up goods line was upgraded to become the up slow line in June 1932, thus making it available to up passenger trains. The up distant signals (Digswell 1 and 6) were with the Welwyn North up starting signal. All the signals at Digswell were originally of the somersault type on wooden posts. When the signal box closed in 1931 these were replaced with upper quadrant arms on lattice posts operated from Welwyn North.

The up home bracket, formerly with two arms (*see* Figure 6.2), was renewed with home arms for the up main and goods lines, each with the Welwyn Garden City outer distant arms below (Welwyn North 16 and 17 formerly Digswell 2 and 7). Under this was a 'calling-on' signal arm (18) for 'permissive working' of goods trains on the up goods line, i.e. allowing more than one train in a block section at the same time. The down home signals (Digswell 12 and 16) formerly carried Welwyn North distants but these were renewed in 1931 with only home signals protecting the junction points. At this time the Welwyn North distant signals were fitted under the Welwyn Garden City down starting signals (25 and 28) and worked by

42

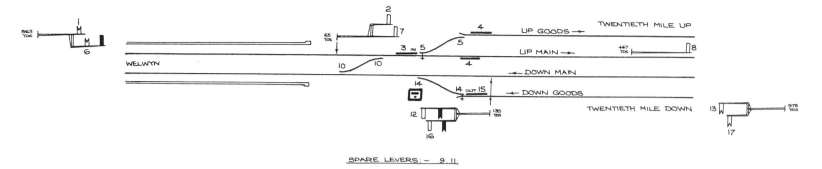

Figure 5.2   *Digswell Junction signal box: 1901 track layout showing position of signals and points with their respective lever numbers*

electric motor. In 1944 colour-light signals ('approach' lit) were installed at Welwyn Garden City incorporating an automatic down distant signal.

The Digswell Junction points, following the abolition of the signal box, were worked by electric motors from Welwyn North, one of the first such installations in the area, but the lack of reliable power supply caused some problems until batteries improved. With the abolition of the Digswell box the crossover points between up and down lines (Digswell 10) were clamped and locked and were for emergency use only.

The up home bracket signal (Welwyn North 16 and 17) was renewed as a colour light signal in 1957 incorporating the Welwyn Garden City up distant signal.

On 20 November 1972 the facing point from the up main to slow line at Digswell Junction was renewed, the facing end being forty yards nearer to Welwyn North while the trailing end was slewed into the up slow line with no catch point. This enabled higher train speeds over the points.

Due to the closure of Welwyn North signal box on 14 September 1973 the points at Digswell Junction were put out of use until 16 September when they again became operational with the new signalling scheme.

Figure 5.3   *Signal lamp from Digswell Junction up home signal (Digswell 2)* © G. Woodward

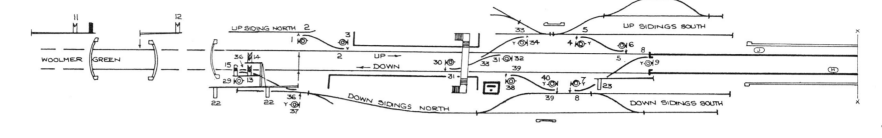

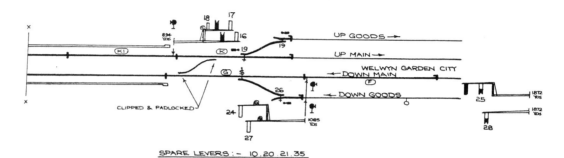

SPARE LEVERS :- 10, 20, 21, 35

5.2 Welwyn North signal box

Figure 5.4 *Welwyn North signal box: 1931 track layout showing position of signals and points with their respective lever numbers*

The up outer distant signal (11) was at the north entrance to Welwyn North Tunnel; the up inner distant (12) was between the tunnels (*see* Figure 5.11) and on a short wooden post with the arm at driver's eye level. Just beyond the southern entrance to Welwyn South Tunnel were two sidings access to which was by reversal from the up line, controlled by points (2) and ground shunting signals (1 and 3). These sidings served a cattle dock until 10 November 1935 when it and the sidings were taken out of use.

The up home signal (15), with a somersault arm just short of the up platform, was a bracket off the down starting signal and hung out over the up track until September 1931 (*see* Figure 3.6) when considerable alterations took place in conjunction with

the abolition of Digswell signal box. These alterations included the fitting of a 40-lever frame in the Welwyn North signal box on 27 September 1931 to take in signals formerly worked by Digswell. Before the alterations the main post had co-acting arms for the down starting signal (22), the bottom section being lattice and the top portion timber. In connection with the 1931 alterations the top timber portion was removed and the signal arm fixed lower down – still giving co-acting arms. The bracket over the up line was lowered to a minimum height and fitted with two dolls to carry the up home (15) and splitting distant arms (13 and 14) indicating the position of the home signals at

signal, because its wire became clogged with soot and dirt from the tunnels and, not being used as often as the main signal, its arm was difficult to get back to the caution position.

It was also unusual to find a set of splitting distant signals with a single-arm home signal (15) between them and the junction signals. In 1957 the Digswell Junction home signal was renewed as a colour-light signal as were the Woolmer Green up starting signal (18)/Welwyn North up outer distant (11) at the north end of the north tunnel. The down home signal (23) at the north end of the viaduct was on a very tall post with co-acting arms and was replaced in 1931 by a short lattice post signal.

There were sidings on both sides of the line at Welwyn North, those on the up side (apart from those serving the cattle dock referred to previously) being south of the station and having two connections to the up and down lines. On the down side (west) the sidings ran behind the down platform and connected

Figure 5.6 *Signalman Horace Ball at work in Welwyn North signal box during 1943*
© *British Railways*

Figure 5.5 *Welwyn North signal box, 17 September 1967*   © *G. W. Goslin*

Digswell Junction. This was one of the first installations of upper quadrant arms in this area.

The up starting signal was originally fixed on to the viaduct over the third arch (*see* Figure 3.4) and also carried the distant arms for Digswell Junction. On the abolition of Digswell box these signals were removed and the former Digswell Junction home signal became the Welwyn North starting signals (16 and 17) with the Welwyn Garden City distant signals below.

The problem of keeping trains moving through this two-track section grew as train speeds increased so an additional routing distant signal was provided beside the up inner distant signal (12) between the tunnels to give an earlier warning to drivers of the route to be taken at Digswell Junction. (*See* Figure 5.8 and 9.1.) Added problems arose with the new routing distant

Figure 5.7   *Signalman Henry Bygrave standing by an open tourer in Welwyn station down-side yard in May 1922. Note the 5-ton crane*   Courtesy of Mrs Christina Hull

(*Above*) Figure 5.8   *The upper quadrant up inner distant signals between the tunnels, July 1963*   © G. W. Goslin

(*Below*) Figure 5.9   *Down starting signals at Welwyn North station (Welwyn North 22) 12 June 1971. Note the rear of the colour light signal relating to the up line*
© H. J. Stull

with the main lines north and south of the platform. The north end points were removed about 1963. All these points and ground signals were controlled from Welwyn North signal box. All sidings were abolished on 31 December 1967, leaving only one crossover between the up and down lines. Welwyn North signal box was switched out on 14 September 1973, pending closure two days later, and demolished in December of that year.

5.3   Woolmer Green signal box

This signal box stood on the up side of the tracks at the end of the up goods line and had twenty-four levers of Saxby and Farmer origin. The up distant signals (20 and 24) were of the somersault type as normally found on the GNR, that relating to the up main line (20) being on a tall post and additionally had an upper quadrant spectacle plate fitted at driver's eye level serving as a repeater for the main arm. This signal latterly had a colour-light distant signal to repeat it and as train speeds rose the colour-light became the main distant signal and the somersault signal was abolished.

The up goods home signal (23) was on a short lattice post, latterly carrying a short upper quadrant arm. The up fast home (19) and down fast starting signals (3 and 9) were renewed on concrete posts in 1925, and the latter signal was provided with

With the new signalling scheme controlled from Kings Cross, Woolmer Green and Knebworth signal boxes were closed on 7 October 1973 and the up goods line between the two places became the up slow line enabling passenger trains to use it.

5.4 Power signalling

The new power signal box at York Road, Kings Cross was put into use during the summer of 1976 when signals and points

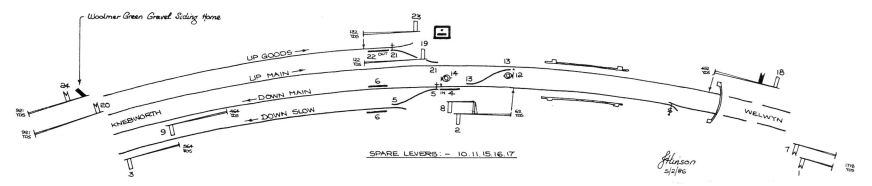

Figure 5.10   *Woolmer Green signal box: 1903 track layout showing position of signals and points with their respective lever numbers*

a white painted sighting panel on the Great North Road bridge wall. The down home bracket signal (2 and 8) was on a very tall timber post and survived until replaced in the main colour-light signal scheme in 1973.

The up starting signal (18) was by the entrance to Welwyn North Tunnel and had the Welwyn North outer distant (Welwyn North 11) under it; in 1957 these were replaced by colour-light signals. The down distant signal was between the tunnels and was a single arm (*see* Figure 5.11), later renewed as a bracket signal (1 and 7) with two somersault arms (*see* Figure 6.4), giving early warning of the home signals to enable goods trains to clear the section more quickly. This was in turn replaced by a colour-light signal in the same configuration. (*See* Figure 6.5.)

covering Hertford North to Gordon Hill, Finsbury Park to Wood Green (now Alexandra Palace) and Holloway were operated from it. At the same time all signals between Kings Cross and a point just south of Grantham had been replaced by three or four-aspect colour-light signals, not all as yet transferred to new control panels. The complete switch-in to Kings Cross came in April 1977, after which it controlled all train movements between Kings Cross and Sandy, between Hitchin and Royston, and between Moorgate and Finsbury Park. The scheme rendered fifty-seven signal boxes redundant including those at Welwyn Garden City, Welwyn North and Woolmer Green.

Most of the present colour-light signals in this area are affixed to a short metal post, the lights (signals) being at driver's eye level, and all on the fast lines can show the four aspects: red – stop, yellow – prepare to find next signal at red, two yellows – prepare to find next signal at yellow, and green – clear. Unusually, the yellow position of the down signal between the tunnels shows a flashing light when indicating that a train is to diverge to the slow line at Woolmer Green. This is instead of the more usual 'feather', i.e. illuminated direction arm, as installed on the up line just south of Welwyn North station to indicate crossing to the slow line at Digswell Junction.

Each signal post has a plate showing a letter K denoting that it is controlled by Kings Cross, followed by a number, by which the signal post is referred to for operating purposes.

As with colour-light signalling elsewhere the signals are audibly repeated in the driver's cab, a bell-ring for green and a hoot for any other signal. If the driver fails to press a button to acknowledge any hoot, the brakes are automatically applied. The necessary trackside apparatus was installed in the area some time before colour-light signalling. This is known as Audible Warning System (AWS).

Figure 5.11　A GNR 2–2–2 on an up express train between the Welwyn tunnels in the post 1903 era. Note the Welwyn up distant somersault signal (Welwyn 12)

© *Photomatic Ltd*

Chapter 6

Express Trains

At the time of the opening of the Great Northern main line from London in August 1850, only seven passenger trains in each direction passed through Welwyn, and of these fourteen no fewer than eleven stopped there. The 7.40 am London to York took 7 hours 10 minutes to cover the 210 miles to York via Boston, Lincoln, Retford, Doncaster and Knottingley. Connections were made at Knottingley for Leeds, at Milford for Hull, and at York for Edinburgh by the York & North Midland Railway; the last journey taking 12 hours. In 1852, when the more direct 'Towns' line via Grantham and Newark-on-Trent was opened, the distance to York was reduced to 190½ miles and the journey time by the 7.40 am to York was reduced to 4 hours 50 minutes.

As traffic expanded over the years more trains were added until, in 1890, some thirty through trains passed Welwyn each way on weekdays serving Nottingham, Sheffield, Manchester, Leeds, Bradford, Newcastle and Scottish destinations.

6.1 Yorkshire and Scottish expresses

Undoubtedly the best known express over the East Coast route was the 10 am from Kings Cross to Edinburgh, inaugurated in 1862 and thereafter running, with only brief breaks due to emergency changes, for 120 years. First known as a 'Special Scotch Express' the train became unofficially known as 'The Flying Scotsman' and officially so named by the LNER after the 1923 grouping. In the summer of 1928 and each year to 1939 this train ran non-stop over the 392¾ miles from Kings Cross to Edinburgh – a world record for a regular service. (*See* Figure 6.2.) The journey time of 8¼ hours in 1928 was progressively reduced to 7 hours in 1937. After enforced breaks during the

war years, non-stop running was restored in 1948, taking 7 hours 50 minutes. In 1949 a new service took over the non-stop running between London and Edinburgh, leaving 'The Flying Scotsman' to make intermediate calls *en route* to Scotland. The new service was first named 'The Capitals Limited' but was changed in 1953 to 'The Elizabethan' and continued as such until 1961. Departure from Kings Cross was at 9.30 am and the journey time reduced to 6¾ hours.

On the outbreak of war in September 1939 drastic reductions were made in all long distance train services in addition to short-lived panic reductions to the inner and outer suburban services. The emergency timetable dated 10 September 1939 provided only four daily trains to Scotland and three to West Yorkshire. This proved totally inadequate for traffic, often making reliefs necessary. Additional trains were put on in December, one each to Edinburgh, West Yorkshire and Hull

Figure 6.1   A pre-1903 view of a GNR 4–2–2 on a London bound train at the south end of the viaduct   *Courtesy of G. W. Goslin*

and three to Newcastle. Even so as many as twenty coaches were needed on many trains, sometimes increased to twenty-four. The heaviest load on record was on Sunday 31 March 1940, when the 10.45 am Newcastle to London left Peterborough with twenty-four main line coaches and two fish vans weighing an unprecedented 764 tons gross, hauled by only one loco-motive, Class V2 2-6-2 No 4800. The 76 miles from Peterborough to Kings Cross took 102 minutes but it was a remarkable feat for a single engine and crew to accomplish and something unheard of on any other British railway at the time. The present InterCity 125 High Speed Trains (HST) consist of seven, mainly eight, or sometimes nine, coaches and two power cars.

Further timetable revisions came in May 1940 when there

Figure 6.2   *LNER Class A1 'Pacific' No 2547* Doncaster *with the up 'Flying Scotsman' non-stop from Edinburgh, at the south end of the viaduct, soon after its re-introduction in 1928*   *Courtesy of D. E. White*

Figure 6.3   *The up 'Silver Jubilee' streamlined express from Newcastle to Kings Cross hauled by an LNER Class A4 'Pacific' No 2509* Silver Link *passing Welwyn Garden City soon after its inauguration in September 1935*
Courtesy of Welwyn Garden City Library

were thirteen express and four semi-fast or stopping trains out of Kings Cross each weekday compared with twenty-five and ten respectively in pre-war 1939.

September 1935 saw the introduction of Britain's first stream-lined train, the 'Silver Jubilee' running between Newcastle and Kings Cross five days a week. This revolutionary train, for which four specially designed locomotives were built together with entirely new coaches whose interior decor set a high stan-dard of comfort, was approached only by two other LNER streamliners introduced in 1937. These were the 'Coronation' to Edinburgh and the 'West Riding Limited' to Leeds and Brad-ford. All these passed through Welwyn at speeds of around 90 mph.

In 1956 two new departures simultaneously from London and Edinburgh at 4 pm were named 'The Talisman'. With only one stop, each journey took 6 hours 40 minutes. Later when 8 am departures both ways were added, the names 'Morning

Figure 6.4 *LNER Class A4 streamlined 'Pacific' No 4492* Dominion of New Zealand *on a Leeds to Kings Cross express between the tunnels in 1938. Note the up inner distant upper quadrant signal (Welwyn North 12) in the foreground and the down distant somersault signals (Woolmer Green 1 and 7)*
Courtesy of Real Photographs Co

Talisman' and 'Afternoon Talisman' were used. Still later, the morning train was extended to Perth becoming 'The Fair Maid', but this service did not last very long.

The first main line diesel-electric locomotive to appear on the Great Northern line, the English Electric 2000 hp Type 4 No D200 (later Class 40), arrived at Welwyn Garden City on a test train of seven coaches from Doncaster on 9 April 1958. On 21 June D201 took out the first diesel-hauled 'Flying Scotsman' from Kings Cross to Newcastle. Henceforth diesel locomotives gradually replaced steam haulage, the ultimate classes being the well-known 3300 hp Class 55 'Deltics' (*see* Figure 6.8) and the more mundane 2750 hp Class 47 Type 4s built by Brush Traction. It was intended that all passenger trains south of Peterborough should be diesel-powered (either locomotive or multiple units) from 17 June 1963 and the final scheduled steam hauled working from Kings Cross was made by Pacific Class

A1 No 60158 *Aberdonian* on the 10.45 pm to Leeds on the previous day. However there were subsequently a large number of isolated steam-hauled trains to and from Kings Cross.

Diesel-electric locomotives started to appear on the outer suburban services in late 1958 and by April 1959 three different types had been allocated to suburban trains (*see* Chapter 11) with varying degrees of success. It was to be late in 1963 before steam haulage was finally discontinued. During the diesel era, diesel multiple-unit sets (DMUs) were used in conjunction with locomotive-hauled trains, principally on the off-peak services.

Diesel haulage of all trains continued until 20 March 1978 when, after numerous test and special runs, the first HST entered regular passenger service on the 0745 from Kings Cross to Edinburgh, at that time named 'Silver Jubilee', returning from the Scottish capital at 1500 hours. This duty had hitherto been entrusted to 'Deltic' diesel-electric locomotives since the inaugural run of the 'Silver Jubilee' on 8 June 1977. Locomotive No 55012 *Crepello* hauled that train complete with appropriate headboard.

The HSTs run in sets comprising seven, but mainly eight or nine passenger coaches of Mark III design with a power car at each end, in which a 2250 hp 12-cylinder diesel engine generates power for the electric motors.

Figure 6.5 *LNER Class B1 4–6–0 No 61394 on an up semi-fast train between the tunnels in 1953*
© *G. W. Goslin*

Figure 6.6   *BR Class A1 'Pacific' No 60122* Curlew *hauling an up express between the tunnels in June 1958. Note the up inner distant signals and the colour light signals on the down line* © G. W. Goslin

The HSTs took over the 'Flying Scotsman' working on 8 May 1978, the last locomotive-hauled run being on the previous Saturday when 'Deltic' No 55010 *The King's Own Scottish Borderer* was used. Deltics continued to work other trains until 31 December 1981. HSTs progressively took over all the daytime main line workings, the programme being completed when they took over the York services in May 1982 and those to Cleethorpes on 4 October 1982. (*See* Plate 6.)

The fastest scheduled timing from Kings Cross to Edinburgh behind a 'Deltic' was 5 hours 27 minutes in 1977 and in the 1984/5 timetable the 1030 hours 'Flying Scotsman' HST covered the 393½ miles in 4½ hours, with a stop at Newcastle. Thus, over the 57 years since 1928 the time taken from Kings Cross to Edinburgh has been reduced from 8¼ hours to 4½ hours – no mean achievement. It is reported that the electric services due to commence in May 1991 will take 4 hours 22 minutes, but with longer trains. The increased mileage from Kings Cross

to Edinburgh, 393½ miles, was the result, *inter alia*, of diversions following the collapse of Penmanshiel Tunnel and the opening of the Selby-avoiding line.

As indicated earlier, many record breaking trains have passed through Welwyn. Recently, on 27 September 1985, a seven-car HST, including power cars 43038 and 43158, ran from Newcastle to Kings Cross at an average speed of 115 mph, setting a new record for the journey of 2 hours 19 minutes 37 seconds. During the run the train reached an unofficial speed of 145 mph.

In conclusion it might be mentioned that the longest service covered by an HST in 1986 is by the noon 'Highland Chieftain' departure from Kings Cross through to Inverness (588 miles), arriving there at 2042, (8 hours 42 minutes). In contrast the 'Clansman' through service from Euston to Inverness (569 miles) takes 9 hours 31 minutes (summer only) in 1986.

6.2   Pullman services

Brief mention should be made of the Great Northern line's Pullman services which have always attracted attention as they sped across the viaduct.

Figure 6.7   *Up passenger train emerging from Welwyn North Tunnel hauled by BR Type 4 (Class 40) 2000 hp diesel-electric locomotive No D201 in June 1958* © G. W. Goslin

The first British dining car, a Pullman vehicle named *Prince of Wales*, entered service on the GNR in 1879 between Kings Cross and Leeds but prior to this, in 1875, Pullman cars were in service between Kings Cross and Manchester and in 1878 two Pullman sleeping cars were running in the overnight trains to Scotland and back. Regular all-Pullman expresses commenced to work between Kings Cross, Leeds, Harrogate and Newcastle in July 1923 and to Sheffield in June 1924, extended to Manchester in April 1925. But the Sheffield/ Manchester service was poorly supported and was withdrawn in favour of a new service from Harrogate, Bradford and Leeds to Kings Cross in September 1925 which as 'The West Riding Pullman' continued until September 1935, when at revised times it became the 'Yorkshire Pullman' until 1939. The Harrogate–Newcastle service was extended to Edinburgh in 1925 and to Glasgow in 1928 when it became 'The Queen of Scots'.

A Sunday Pullman service commenced in July 1927 when the 'Harrogate Sunday Pullman' was introduced between Kings Cross and Harrogate via Leeds. This service continued until September 1939, being restored in June 1950. The train was finally withdrawn in October 1968.

In November 1946 the popular 'Yorkshire Pullman' was restored, the inaugural trips being made by specially refurbished Gresley A3 Pacifics Nos 97 *Humorist* and 107 *Royal Lancer*, both carrying lined green livery and named headboards on their smokebox fronts. This service had to be suspended in the winter due to a severe coal supply crisis and was not restored until October 1947.

A second Pullman service, the 'Queen of Scots', between London and Glasgow was restored in July 1948 and in September an entirely new Pullman service started named 'Tees–Tyne Pullman' from Newcastle to Kings Cross and return, arriving at 2.16 pm and returning at 5.30 pm. This approximated to the pre-war 'Silver Jubilee' streamlined service.

In the 1958 winter timetable a new Pullman service between Kings Cross and Sheffield was introduced under the title

Figure 6.8   *BR 'Deltic' diesel-electric locomotive No. D9020* Nimbus *hauling the down centenary 'Flying Scotsman' on 18 June 1962, passing Holloway South down signal box*
© *J. F. Aylard*

'Master Cutler' and intended for all-diesel haulage, but in the event, steam locomotives were frequently used because of the unreliability of diesel locomotives at that time.

An interesting sight through Welwyn North on 16 October 1965 was the appearance of one of the London Midland Region's six-coach diesel-powered Blue Pullman multiple units. The occasion was a high speed trial from Leeds to Kings Cross and back. Perhaps even more unusual was the test run from Kings Cross to Grantham by Southern Region Diesel-Electric Multiple Unit (DEMU) No 1001 on 6 January 1968.

All locomotive-hauled Pullman services ceased running in the Eastern Region in May 1978. However, in 1985 two HSTs were refurbished and repainted in the latest InterCity livery and with a Pullman-style service in the first class coaches. They became the 'Yorkshire Pullman' between Kings Cross and Leeds, and the 'Tees–Tyne Pullman' between the capital and Newcastle.

Chapter 7

Passenger Services at Welwyn North

For seventy years after the railway was built Welwyn was the largest single settlement between Hatfield and Stevenage. Moreover several influential families resided in the fine estates that characterised much of the Mimram valley. It is not surprising, therefore, that in 1852 nine of the twelve down (northbound) weekday passenger trains from London and all three Sunday trains stopped at Welwyn. Since then Welwyn has grown, although less than other villages and towns on the line. In 1986, for example, 38 out of 109 down passenger trains called there on each weekday. Services from Mondays to Fridays are more frequent than at weekends and are therefore discussed separately in the sub-sections that follow.

7.1 Monday to Friday services

During the nineteenth century many improvements were made to the up and down business trains. When services started in 1850 six trains stopped at Welwyn in each direction. By 1887 the number had increased to twelve up and ten down services and by 1900 to twelve each way. As shown in Table 7.1 this had increased further to fourteen up and thirteen down trains by 1910 when a further up train stopped on request to set down passengers from Peterborough. Despite the intervention of the First World War the service had changed little by 1923 when the GNR became part of the LNER.

By 1937/8 the up service had been increased to eighteen trains. However there were mid-day and mid-evening intervals in the service of over 2⅓ hours each. Further, the 4.31 pm departure, which ended another long interval of 1¾ hours, took 75 minutes to reach Kings Cross. During these long gaps however, Welwyn North was busy with long coal trains passing from Peterborough to London. (*See* Chapter 9.)

Table 7.1 *The number of daily train services and the fastest train(s) on Mondays to Fridays between Welwyn North and London, 1850–1986*

	The Up (Southbound) Services				The Down (Northbound) Services			
Year	*Number of trains*	*Dep. time of fastest service(s) from Welwyn North*	*Time taken (min.)*	*Intermediate calls*	*Number of trains*	*Dep. time of fastest service(s) from London*	*Time taken (min.)*	*Intermediate calls*
1850	6	1.11 pm	49	HA NB	6	12 noon 2 pm 5 pm 8 pm	62	All stations
1862	8	8.37 pm	43	HA NB	9	5.5 pm	47	NB PB HA
1874	10	9.1 am	39	HA HO	8	5.5 pm	45	HA
1884	13	4.2 pm	36	HA FP	10	7 pm	38	FP HA
1890	12	12.8 pm	37	HA FP	9	5 pm	36	HA
1900	12	9.1 am	33	HA FP	12	5.10 pm	32	HA
1910	14	8.22 am	32	FP	13	5.10 pm	32	HA
1920	12[a]	8.22 am 9.1 am	33 33	FP HA FP	12	5.10 pm	35	HA
1930	14[b]	8.24 am	32	FP	17[c]	5.10 pm	33	HA
1940	17	7.43 am 8.24 am	35 35	WGC FP WGC FP	21	5.10 pm	40	HA
1950	27	6.54 am 8.22 am	36 36	WGC FP WGC FP	23	5.39 pm	39	FP WGC
1960	26	7.3 am	34	WGC FP	21	5.10 pm	31	WGC
1970	27	0712 0732	32 32	WGC FP WGC HA FP	23	1743	30	FP
1980	38	0835	25	FP	37	1713	26	FP WGC
1982	38	many	30	WGC HA PB FP	37	many	29	FP PB HA WGC
1986	40	0805	23	FP	37	nine	29	FP PB HA WGC

NOTES: (a) plus one terminating at Hatfield.
           (b) plus two terminating at Welwyn Garden City and one at Hatfield.
           (c) plus three starting from Hatfield and one from Welwyn Garden City.
           FP Finsbury Park; HA Hatfield; HO Holloway; NB New Barnet; PB Potters Bar; WGC Welwyn Garden City.

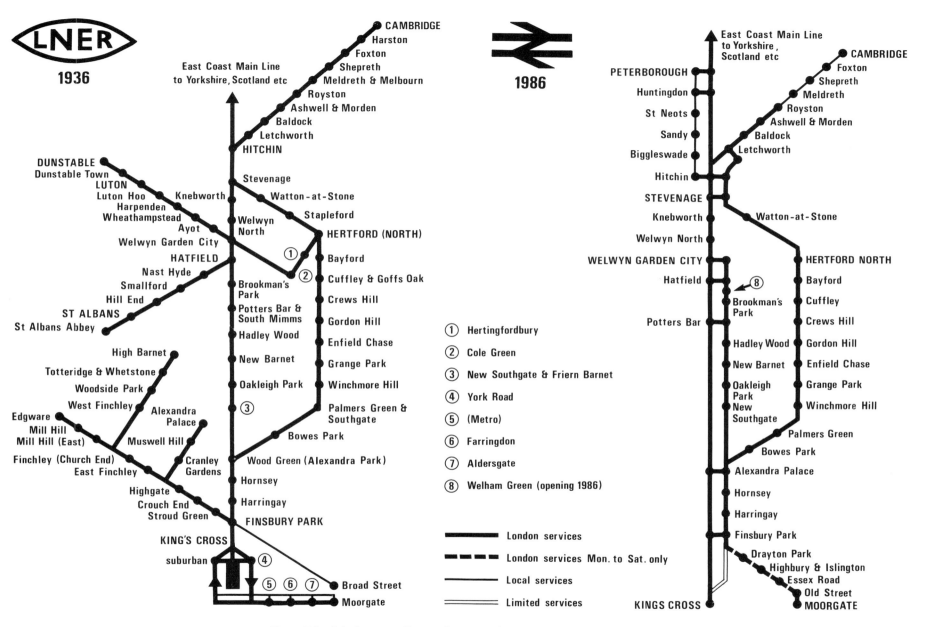

LNER

1936

CAMBRIDGE
Harston
Foxton
Shepreth
Meldreth & Melbourn
Royston
Ashwell & Morden
Baldock
Letchworth
HITCHIN

East Coast Main Line
to Yorkshire, Scotland etc

Stevenage

DUNSTABLE
Dunstable Town
LUTON
Luton Hoo
Harpenden
Wheathampstead
Ayot
Welwyn Garden City
HATFIELD
Nast Hyde
Smallford
Hill End
ST ALBANS
St Albans Abbey

Knebworth

Welwyn
North

Watton-at-Stone

Stapleford

HERTFORD (NORTH)

① Bayford

② Cuffley & Goffs Oak

Crews Hill

Gordon Hill

Enfield Chase

Grange Park

Winchmore Hill

Palmers Green &
Southgate

Bowes Park

High Barnet
Totteridge & Whetstone
Woodside Park
West Finchley
Edgware
Mill Hill
Mill Hill (East)
Finchley (Church End)
East Finchley
Highgate
Crouch End
Stroud Green

Brookman's
Park
Potters Bar &
South Mimms
Hadley Wood

New Barnet

Oakleigh Park

③

Alexandra
Palace

Muswell Hill

Cranley
Gardens

Wood Green (Alexandra Park)

Hornsey

Harringay

FINSBURY PARK

KING'S CROSS
suburban ④

⑤ ⑥ ⑦ Broad Street
Moorgate

① Hertingfordbury
② Cole Green
③ New Southgate & Friern Barnet
④ York Road
⑤ (Metro)
⑥ Farringdon
⑦ Aldersgate
⑧ Welham Green (opening 1986)

━━━━━ London services
╍╍╍╍ London services Mon. to Sat. only
───── Local services
═════ Limited services

1986

East Coast Main Line
to Yorkshire,
Scotland etc

PETERBOROUGH
Huntingdon
St Neots
Sandy
Biggleswade
Hitchin
STEVENAGE
Knebworth
Welwyn North
WELWYN GARDEN CITY
Hatfield

CAMBRIDGE
Foxton
Shepreth
Meldreth
Royston
Ashwell & Morden
Baldock
Letchworth

Watton-at-Stone

HERTFORD NORTH
Bayford
Cuffley
Crews Hill
Gordon Hill
Enfield Chase
Grange Park
Winchmore Hill

⑧

Potters Bar

Brookman's
Park
Hadley Wood
New Barnet
Oakleigh
Park
New
Southgate

Palmers Green
Bowes Park
Alexandra Palace
Hornsey
Harringay
Finsbury Park
Drayton Park
Highbury & Islington
Essex Road
Old Street
MOORGATE

KINGS CROSS

Figure 7.1 *Suburban route diagrams for 1936 and 1986. The route diagram based
on that published in the* LNER Local Timetable 1936 *(left) and that published in
the 1986 BR Great Northern Electric Timetable (right)*

On the outbreak of war in September 1939 services were cut to what soon proved to be inadequate levels. However, when it became clear that extensive bombing was not imminent many trains were restored. By December 1939 the down service to Welwyn North comprised 22 irregularly spaced trains. For example, the 7 pm from Kings Cross was quickly followed by the 7.5 pm and after the 9.25 pm there was only one more departure, at 9.35 pm. In the up direction the 10.33 pm departure for Kings Cross was withdrawn early in 1940. Thus the last train to London at that time departed at 8.22 pm.

In 1941, partly as a result of the wartime evacuation of railway offices to Whitwell and Knebworth, the up service was increased from seventeen to 22 trains daily, and to 24 in the following year. Apart from changes to the morning peak period services (*see* Chapter 8), a serious attempt was made to reduce the intervals between trains and to provide an approximately hourly service throughout the day. This was the start of a regular-interval service at Welwyn North. However, wartime conditions enforced easier timings and, despite some improvements after the war, steam train schedules never again achieved the standards established in 1900.

Diesel locomotives and diesel multiple units (DMUs) replaced steam during the five years commencing August 1958. Although providing 26 up trains daily the timetable did not change fundamentally except for the acceleration of many down trains. Continuing the trend started in 1941 there was an approximately hourly off peak service although some longer intervals remained. A notorious gap in 1970 was between the 1910 and 2035 trains from Kings Cross.

On 8 November 1976 the inner suburban services were electrified using Class 313 EMUs. (*See* Chapter 10.) These ran from Moorgate to Welwyn Garden City and Hertford North via Essex Road and a new link from Drayton Park to Finsbury Park. The services from Broad Street, and from Moorgate via Farringdon, to Finsbury Park and beyond were withdrawn. At this stage Welwyn North was not affected as its service to Moorgate had ceased in about 1903 and its Broad Street service, latterly 'Satur-

days Only', was withdrawn in the early 1960s. Whilst prior to 1976 the GN inner suburban services to Moorgate ran into platforms 5 and 6 situated just below street level, the new electrified services terminated in and started from platforms 9 and 10 at a much deeper level. Platforms 5 and 6 were subsequently used solely by the Bedford line services.

The new service to Moorgate eased pressure on Kings Cross enabling British Railways to carry out a major realignment of the station trackwork in February and March 1977. A special timetable was introduced for the period of this work when many trains terminated at Kings Cross (York Road) and reversed at Moorgate's platforms 5 and 6. This avoided shunting these trains at Kings Cross and thus minimised disruption of the track work. The trains used had to be formed of stock which could be run round the sharp curves of the Moorgate route and more of the locomotive-hauled non-gangwayed coaches appeared on Welwyn North services than ever before. (*See* Chapter 11.)

Following the delivery of more Class 313 trains, peak period semi-fast services were introduced from Welwyn Garden City to Moorgate on 2 May 1977. These were of particular benefit to passengers to and from Potters Bar and Hatfield and following their introduction peak period Welwyn North trains no longer stopped at these stations. As a result the 0718 briefly held a new southbound record schedule of 30 minutes to Kings Cross even though the Welwyn North services had not then been electrified.

Welwyn North's first full electric services commenced on 6 February 1978 using Class 312 EMUs. (*See* Chapter 10 and Timetable in Appendix B6.) These brought a complete transformation of the service including much accelerated timings. The 24 daily southbound trains were increased to 38 and off-peak trains doubled in frequency to run half-hourly. They proved clean, quiet, smooth and reliable, and all ran at speeds previously attained only by the occasional 'flyer'. (*See* Plate 4.) The standard timing between Kings Cross and Welwyn North was 30 minutes which required 80 to 90 mph running between stops. For the first time ever all trains serving Welwyn North were identical,

Plate 5   *Exterior view of the main buildings at Welwyn North station, 18 July 1959*
© *D. E. White*

having first and second class accommodation with shared toilet facilities. Initially the new off-peak outer suburban trains to and from Kings Cross called only at Welwyn Garden City, Hatfield, Potters Bar and Finsbury Park. Since May 1986 most off-peak trains have also called at Alexandra Palace (formerly Wood Green). Further, since May 1985 alternate trains in the down direction have terminated at Letchworth instead of continuing to Royston.

The first major peak-period revisions to the post-electrification timetable took effect in October 1982 when several inner suburban trains were withdrawn, and Hatfield and Potters Bar stops were added to all Welwyn North services which would then, it was predicted, convey 94 passengers per 100 seats. The object was to make financial savings. As a result of the changes trains became overcrowded when Potters Bar passengers transferred from the inner to the outer suburban services. The congestion and longer journey times were claimed by outer suburban passengers to have significantly reduced the quality of travel afforded them. The Class 313 units which were surplus to GN requirements as a result of the timetable changes were transferred to services between Clacton and Colchester, Euston/ Broad Street and Watford Junction and, temporarily, between St Pancras and Bedford.

The number of passengers arriving at Finsbury Park and Kings Cross in each hourly interval was obtained by BR from a survey which unfortunately did not include calculation of the utilisation of individual trains. Although the last two trains to run non-stop from Finsbury Park to Welwyn Garden City were the 1710 and 1730 from Kings Cross, it was later found that the decelerated 1810 carried more than twice as many passengers to Welwyn North as had the 1710. The 1840 from Kings Cross, also a heavily used train, was cut from eight to four coaches but restored to its original length in January 1983 as a result of public representations. In 1985 it was again reduced to four coaches but this time additional trains were also provided at 1830 and 1834. (*See* Chapter 8.) Although these additional trains did not serve Welwyn North they did relieve the congestion on the 1840.

The next major revision of the timetable in May 1985 was in response to a one-day survey of the utilisation of all suburban trains individually at all stations. It brought some peak-period improvements and some economies including the termination of alternate trains at Letchworth thus saving the last quiet 10½ miles to Royston. The new Moorgate/Kings Cross, Fenchurch Street and Liverpool Street suburban timetables were written by a solitary, overworked, official in an unattractive office off Bishopsgate.

Apart from an early morning unadvertised Class 313 staff train which called at Welwyn North on request only, the uniformity of train type ceased on Tuesday 1 October 1985. BR had introduced a down Class 313 train from Moorgate, calling at all stations to arrive at Welwyn North at 0004 on Tuesdays to Sundays. This was the first scheduled train from Moorgate to Welwyn North in the twentieth century. This train had the further distinction of being that used to introduce driver-only

Table 7.2 *The fastest trains between Welwyn North and Kings Cross according to the form of motive power and operator, 1850–1986*

Form of motive power	Operator	Southbound = Up			Northbound = Down		
		Year(s)	Time taken min.	Dep. time from Welwyn North	Year(s)	Time taken min.	Dep. time from Kings Cross
Steam	GNR	1910	32	8.22 am	1900–1916	32	5.10 pm
	LNER	1927–1931	32	8.24 am	1937	32	Saturdays 12.30, 12.54 pm
	BR	1948–1952	36	various e.g. 8.22 am	1952–1958	35	5.52 pm
Diesel	BR	1977	30	0718	1971	26	1804
Electric	BR	1986	23	0805	1978–1980	26	various e.g. 1713

operation to Welwyn North in late November 1985. It was a 'theatre special' augmenting a Kings Cross to Royston train which was changed to run non-stop from Potters Bar, where the two trains connected, to Stevenage. The faster train provided a new late service connecting at Hitchin for stations to St Neots.

In 1852 (*see* Timetable in Appendix B1) scarcely twenty trains in total passed each way daily. In 1986 there are some 280 movements through Welwyn North on each weekday. These include newspaper, parcel and goods, as well as passenger, services. In 1986 the busiest hour in the up direction is from 0745 to 0845 when twelve trains, of which five stop at Welwyn North, pass through the 'bottleneck'. The pathing of these trains was simplified by the fact that all overnight trains should have passed by this time and the InterCity business services have yet to follow. However, peak-period services may be disrupted when overnight trains are delayed. This is a long-standing problem. As long ago as 1933 a circular directed to the signal boxes at Welwyn North and Woolmer Green stated that 'it is agreed to the Up Outer Suburban peak hour trains taking turns with the Up Scotch Expresses . . . when the latter are running more than 15 minutes late south of Hitchin'.

The busiest hour in the down direction in 1986 was 1740 to 1840 when thirteen trains, of which three called, passed Welwyn North. These include some prestige services such as 'The Yorkshire Pullman'. Long-distance trains are generally given priority through the 'bottleneck' as generations of travellers to Welwyn North have experienced whilst waiting at Welwyn Garden City station or Digswell Junction.

For travellers to Welwyn North from Stevenage and other more northerly employment, education and shopping centres, the present half-hourly service is sufficient. In the past there was a generally less frequent service with extra trains being provided during the peak periods. A surprise in May 1986 was the addition to the half-hourly sequence of an extra up train doubling as a 'theatre' special. This departed from Welwyn North at 1759 and ran non-stop from Welwyn Garden City to Finsbury Park. Not for 96 years had an afternoon train from

Welwyn North been scheduled to reach Kings Cross with only two intermediate stops.

Since 1979, one, and sometimes two, of Welwyn North's down morning services have varied from the general half-hourly pattern to connect at Stevenage with down InterCity trains. Thus, for example, a journey time of 121 minutes from Welwyn North to Leeds became possible in 1983/4.

7.2 Weekend services

In response to the 5½-day week worked in some offices, the earlier timetables show various down mid-day 'Saturdays Only' trains. One, which ran for several years, left Kings Cross at 12.40 pm and ran non-stop to Knebworth. Between 1918 and May 1919 it started calling at Welwyn providing, in 34 minutes, the earliest known London–Welwyn non-stop service. By 1937 there were two fast mid-day trains. Both the 12.30 and 12.54 pm from Kings Cross ran non-stop to Welwyn Garden City, reaching Welwyn North in 32 minutes. By comparison, in the same year, no train left London for Welwyn North on Mondays to Fridays between 11.30 am and 1.3 pm. The latter took 60 minutes for the journey. Late-night travellers were also especially provided for at weekends. For example, in 1940 the 12.20 am seven nights per week inner suburban train to Welwyn Garden City was extended to serve Welwyn North on Saturday and Sunday nights only.

After the Second World War, offices began to close altogether on Saturdays, and the 'extras' were progressively withdrawn during the late 1950s and mid 1960s. The last surviving Saturday train additional to the normal off-peak service was the 0820 from Welwyn North to Kings Cross, which made its last run on 30 May 1981.

Outside the peak periods, Saturday services have usually been the same as from Mondays to Fridays, originally being included in a 'Weekdays' section of the timetables and individually annotated 'Saturdays Only', as appropriate. Since 11

September 1961, however, the timetables for Mondays to Fridays and Saturdays have been printed in separate sections. The 24-hour clock was adopted from 14 June 1965.

Sunday services have always been set out in separate sections of the timetables. In Britain Sunday trains have traditionally been relatively infrequent and slow. By comparison most other European countries run almost identical services seven days a week. From 1850 to 1922, the usual Sunday service at Welwyn comprised two up and three down trains. Of the down trains, two ran in the morning and the third about nine hours later. There were however a few exceptions. In 1887, for example, there were one morning, and two evening trains which ran only 28 minutes apart. In 1910 there were two morning and two evening down trains and a mid-afternoon service, calling at Welwyn at 4.46 pm, operated by the single coach Ivatt Steam Motor Car. (*See* Chapter 10.)

The up Sunday service during the years 1850 to 1922 comprised a morning train leaving Welwyn between 8.48 am and 9 am and an evening train departing between 7.16 and 7.28 pm. In most years this was the entire up Sunday service.

For a brief period in 1852 the 10.20 am all-stations from York to Kings Cross called at Welwyn at 6.48 pm, and in 1910 the Steam Motor Car provided a third up service departing at 4.14 pm for Hatfield only. This was replaced in 1914 by a locomotive-hauled train departing at 5.36 pm for Kings Cross.

Between 1922 and 1939, as already noted, the Mondays to Fridays service increased from thirteen to eighteen in the up and to 22 in the down direction daily. The Sunday service, however, was increased from three to eleven trains. This was further increased in the two years after the Second World War (1946/7) to sixteen up and fifteen down. This level of service was approximately maintained until 1958. In the early 1960s the service became a strictly hourly one. The first up train, however, the 0545 departure from Letchworth in the 1986 timetable, although calling at Stevenage, Knebworth, and Welwyn Garden City, etc. in most years omitted Welwyn North.

Electrification in 1978 brought an even more frequent Sunday service to Welwyn North. A total of 31 up and 32 down trains ran hourly in the early morning and half hourly for the rest of the day. However, engineering work, frequently needed between Woolmer Green and Digswell Junction, is usually carried out on Sundays. In this event all services to and from stations north from Stevenage may be re-routed via Hertford North and buses chartered from local operators and titled 'Railway Emergency Service' used to transport passengers between Stevenage, Knebworth, Welwyn North and Welwyn Garden City.

In October 1981 both the inner and outer suburban Sunday services were halved. However the hourly trains to and from Welwyn North made additional calls at New Barnet and Oakleigh Park, thus maintaining a half-hourly service at these busier stations.

Chapter 8
Principal Peak Period Passenger Services

The timetables for the peak periods at Welwyn North show a remarkable consistency from year to year, with many services running at much the same times for several decades. This is evident from Tables 8.1 and 8.2 which list all the morning up and evening down peak period services between Welwyn North and London for selected years between 1852 and 1986. For the purposes of the present work, peak period trains have been defined as those due to arrive in London between 0700 and 1000 hours, and those due to leave London for Welwyn North between 1600 and 1900 hours. Although this chapter deals essentially with services between Welwyn and London, not all up trains have terminated there. For example, between 1931 and 1937 departures from Welwyn North at 7.33 am and 8.13/8.14 am terminated at Hatfield and Welwyn Garden City respectively.

In catering for the morning southbound and the evening northbound peak periods different considerations apply. In the morning the commuter has a notional time for arriving at work and selects an appropriate train. The train departure time may then determine the household breakfast routine. Further, as the spread of these notional target times is quite narrow, it is usually sufficient to provide just one or two 'fast' trains from each station. Subject to such provision being made, there may be little need for fundamental changes in the timetable from one year to the next, and some stability in the pattern of services is to be expected. None the less, the present authors in researching for this book were surprised by its extent. For example the departure times from Welwyn North of two morning trains, the 0812 and 0856 in the 1986 timetable, have never been varied by more than nine minutes. In contrast, the exigencies of work may unpredictably detain the commuter in the evening, with the result that there is a broader spread of travel patterns than in the morning. For example, a service interval of 46 minutes (51 minutes at Welwyn North) in 1950 led to a petition which the *Welwyn Times*, in the measured prose of those days, reported as requesting 'that urgent attention be given to remedying the present unsatisfactory situation', and a correspondent, equally decorously, feared that 'much of the goodwill between the Railway Executive and local residents . . . is in danger of being lost'. As the evening traffic is less predictable and is spread over more hours than that in the morning, the demand is too diffuse to justify fast trains to the smaller stations. Thus since 1982 all Kings Cross to Welwyn North trains have made at least four intermediate stops. The pattern of services has been subject to significant year-to-year variations. However one northbound Welwyn North train, often referred to as 'the 5.5 pm' (Johns 1939), has retained a continuous identity since Welwyn station opened in August 1850. Its departure time has never been varied by more than ten minutes at a time and it left Kings Cross at exactly 5.10 pm for over fifty years from 1900. On inception in 1850 its departure time was 5 pm and in 1986 it was 1708.

8.1 The up services

The up (southbound) service shows numerous consistent features over several decades. Since 1906 it seems there has always been an arrival at Kings Cross from Welwyn North in each of the periods 0838 to 0848, 0858 to 0904, and 0926 to 0942. Further, since 1942, the first train has always arrived at Kings Cross at about 0630 and the second train has always arrived between 0653 and 0711. Indeed, of the southbound peak period

Table 8.1 Schedule of morning peak period services from Welwyn North (formerly Welwyn) to London (arriving between 0700 and 1000 hours) for selected years 1852–1986

Departure time from Welwyn/Welwyn North (top) / Arrival time in London (bottom)

Commencement date of timetable	First train									
August 1852	0756 / 0900	0756 Z / 0900								0900 Z / 1000
1 January 1858	0757 / 0900	0757 / 0900								0842 / 0930
November 1862	0757 / 0900	0757 / 0900								0838 / 0932
March 1874	0741 / 0842	0741 / 0842						0836 / 0901		0901 / 0940
January 1884	0700 / 0814 Moorgate	0700 Z / 0814 Moorgate						0841 H / 0930		0904 K / 0945
1 June 1890	0659 / 0800	0659 Z / 0800					0801 K / 0843	0841 H / 0930		0904 K / 0945
1 October 1900	0651 / 0808 Moorgate	0651 Z / 0808 Moorgate					0801 M / 0844			0901 G / 0934 L
1 July 1907	0658 / 0745	0658 Z / 0745					0801 / 0840	0822 A / 0855		0901 G / 0934
12 July 1915	0658 / 0743	0658 Z / 0743					0801 / 0840	0822 A / 0855		0901 G / 0934
3 October 1921	0639 / 0727	0639 Z / 0727					0801 H / 0841	0822 A / 0855		0901 G / 0934
26 September 1927	0628 / 0725	0628 Z / 0725					0758 K / 0835	0824 A / 0856		0901 G / 0934
1 May 1931	0628 / 0725	0717 / 0757	0628 Z / 0725				0757 K / 0835	0824 A / 0856		0901 G / 0934
27 September 1937	0627 / 0722	0717 / 0757	0627 Z / 0722				0757 K / 0835	0824 A / 0856		0901 G / 0934
6 October 1941	0538 / 0638	0651 C / 0729	0715 C / 0751	0725 / 0808	0743 C / 0818	0802 D / 0847	0824 C / 0859	0842 C / 0921		0858 D / 0942
January 1947	0531 / 0633	0617 / 0708	0649 C / 0730	0713 C / 0751	0723 / 0813	0742 C / 0818	0756 F / 0846	0818 C / 0856	0841 C / 0923	0853 D / 0938
30 June 1952	0529 / 0634	0617 / 0708	0654 C / 0731	0720 / 0812	0744 C / 0822	0800 H / 0848	0822 C / 0858	0845 C / 0923		0857 D / 0940
1 December 1958	0528 / 0632	0614 Z / 0716	0655 C / 0734	0720 / 0812	0742 C / 0822	0800 H / 0848	0821 C / 0859	0845 C / 0922		0857 D / 0939
7 September 1964	0543 / 0639	0614 Z / 0704	0706 C / 0742	0720 / 0809	0737 C / 0814	0805 J / 0844	0823 C / 0901	0849 C / 0922		0858 D / 0936
5 May 1969	0545 / 0637	0614 Z / 0702	0712 C / 0744	0732 C / 0804	0747 C / 0820	0806 J / 0842	0828 C / 0901	0848 F / 0927		0901 D / 0935
1 May 1972	0556 / 0646	0619 Z / 0709	0704 T / 0744	0732 R / 0807	0741 E / 0819	0809 J / 0844	0830 C / 0903	0849 F / 0930		0905 D / 0942
5 May 1975	0555 / 0646	0621 Z / 0711	0705 T / 0744	0730 R / 0804	0739 E / 0815	0804 J / 0840	0830 C / 0902	0851 F / 0929		0905 D / 0942
2 May 1977	0557 / 0635	0634 F / 0711	0703 C / 0734	0718 B / 0748	0733 C / 0804	0811 C / 0843	0833 C / 0903			0906 F / 0943
6 February 1978	0607 / 0636	0637 F / 0706	0704 C / 0729	0734 C / 0800	0754 C / 0820	0814 A / 0840	0834 A / 0900			0907 F / 0936
1 June 1981	0602 / 0631	0632 F / 0701	0702 F / 0731	0732 E / 0759	0752 D / 0819	0812 D / 0839	0836 A / 0900			0908 F / 0938
4 October 1982	0557 / 0627	0657 F / 0729	0727 F / 0759	0750 F / 0821	0814 F / 0845	0825 C / 0859	0834 C / 0911	0842 C / 0913	0857 F / 0933	0927 F / 1000
3 October 1983	0557 / 0627	0657 F / 0729	0727 F / 0759	0750 F / 0821	0814 C / 0845	0830 C / 0901	0840 C / 0901		0857 F / 0933	0927 F / 1000
13 May 1985	0558 / 0630	0658 C / 0725	0728 F / 0759	0750 F / 0822	0801 A / 0825	0813 F / 0843	0830 F / 0901	0839 F / 0910	0858 F / 0929	0928 F / 0958
12 May 1986	0554 / 0623	0656 C / 0722	0726 C / 0755	0747 F / 0817	0805 A / 0828	0812 F / 0842	0830 C / 0903	0842 F / 0912	0856 F / 0926	0924 F / 0957

NOTES

A Non-stop to Finsbury Park
B Non-stop from Welwyn Garden City and Finsbury Park
C Called Welwyn Garden City and Finsbury Park
D As C plus Hatfield

E As C plus Potters Bar
F As C plus Hatfield and Potters Bar
G Called Hatfield and Finsbury Park
H Stations to Hadley Wood or New Barnet and Finsbury Park
J As C or D plus Brookmans Park
K Called at Hatfield, Potters Bar and Finsbury Park
L Horses not conveyed
M Horses not conveyed to certain stations

R Called at Welwyn Garden City and Hatfield
T As C plus Hatfield, Brookmans Park and Potters Bar.
Z Called at all, or most, intermediate stations

Table 8.2 Schedule of evening peak period services from London (between 1600 and 1900 hours) to Welwyn North (formerly Welwyn) for selected years 1852–1986

Commencement date of timetable	Departure time from London (King's Cross unless otherwise stated) / Arrival time at Welwyn/Welwyn North									Last train
August 1852	1600 Z / 1702		1700 Z / 1753				1800 Z / 1853			2000 / 2053
1 February 1858	1600 Z / 1701		1703 A / 1739				1805 Z / 1906			1945 / 2045
April 1864	1600		1705 / 1759				1800			2000 / 2105
March 1874			1705 / 1750				1805			1839 / 2036
January 1884			1708 / 1754		1745 Slip coach for Potters Bar / 1824				1900 F / 1938	2033 / 2120
1 June 1890			1700 A / 1736 D		1750 G / 1833 D			1830 (Moorgate 1817) / 1922 Z		2040 / 2129
1 October 1900		1630 G / 1710	1700 A / 1742		1748 K / 1828			1818 D / 1859 F	1900 F / 1938	2205 / 2244
1 October 1906		1638 → Hertford 1710 E G	1710 A / 1742 M		1749 K / 1828			1818 D / 1859 F	1900 F / 1938	2200 N / 2243
12 July 1915		1630 G / 1710 E	1710 A / 1742		1749 K / 1834			1818 D / 1859 F	1900 F / 1938	2145 / 2227
5 May 1919	1615 → Grantham 1707 E G		1710 A / 1745		1749 / 1828			1815 / 1856		2200 / 2246
July 1922	1615 → Grantham 1707 E G		1710 A / 1743		1750 K / 1832			1830 F / 1908	1900 F / 1943	2300 N / 2338
1 May 1931	1615 E / 1709		1710 E / 1743	1734 B / 1809			1802 Q / 1838	1830 R / 1912	1855 H / 1941	2345 / 0035
27 September 1937	1615 E / 1708 H		1710 A / 1743	1735 B / 1810			1802 Q / 1838	1830 R / 1911	1852 H / 1950	2345 / 0036
6 October 1941	1620 / 1708	1645 / 1734	1710 / 1752	1734 / 1816	1748 / 1835		1810 R / 1857	1825 / 1912	1857 / 1956	2155 / 2243
1 October 1945	1624 / 1707	1650 / 1738	1710 T / 1749	1734 Q / 1815			1810 R / 1855	1820 R / 1907	1840 R / 1925	2235 / 2338
20 September 1950	1621 H / 1704	Broad St 1643 / 1736	1710 T / 1752		1739 Q / 1818			1825 R / 1909	1840 H / 1923	2321 / 0002
December 1958	1621 P / 1709	Broad St 1638 / 1737	1712 T / 1757		1739 Q / 1819	1752 C / 1827		1820 R / 1908	1849 P / 1933	2325 / 0041
7 December 1959	1625 P / 1707		1710 B / 1741		1740 Q / 1813	1752 C / 1824		1817 T / 1900	1839 P / 1921	2325 / 0010
9 September 1963	1622 P / 1702		1715 B / 1746		1741 Q / 1814	1752 C / 1822		1817 T / 1851	1839 P / 1922	2325 / 0006
6 March 1967	1621 P / 1704		1714 Non-stop / 1742		1739 Buffet Non-stop / 1807		1804 B / 1835	1835 T / 1908		0003 / 0054
3 May 1971	1619 P / 1700		1718 B / 1748		1744 Q / 1816		1804 Non-stop / 1830	1830 T / 1903		2328 / 0008
8 November 1976	1615 H / 1654			1725 B / 1756; 1727 H / 1809	1745 B / 1815		1804 B / 1835	1818 B / 1850	1840 / 1917	2330 / 0009
6 February 1978	1618 H / 1648	1651 Q / 1718	1712 Q / 1739	1729 Q / 1755	1751 Q / 1817		1812 Q / 1838		1848 H / 1917	2348 / 0017
17 May 1982	1610 H / 1640	1640 H / 1710	1710 Q / 1739	1730 Q / 1758	1748 H / 1818		1810 H / 1839		1840 H / 1910	2350 / 0019
4 October 1982	1610 H / 1639	1640 H / 1710	1708 H / 1738	1733 H / 1804	1748 H / 1818		1810 H / 1839		1840 H / 1910	2350 / 0019
12 May 1986	1610 J / 1641	1640 H / 1709	1708 H / 1737	1734 H / 1807	1748 H / 1818		1810 H / 1839		1840 J / 1911	2359 / 0028

NOTES
A Called at Hatfield only
B Called at Welwyn Garden City only
C Called at Finsbury Park only
D Train divided at Hatfield: front portion non-stop to Hitchin, rear portion all stations to Hitchin
E Change at Hatfield
F Called Finsbury Park, Hadley Wood, Potters Bar and Hatfield
G As F plus Potters Bar
H Calls Finsbury Park, Potters Bar, Hatfield and Welwyn Garden City
J As H plus Alexandra Palace
K Called at Finsbury Park and Hatfield
M Horses and Carriages not conveyed Wednesdays
N An additional train ran at midnight on Wednesdays
P As H plus Brookmans Park
Q Called at Finsbury Park and Welwyn Garden City only
R As Q plus Hatfield
T Called at Hatfield and Welwyn Garden City only
Z Called all stations

trains running in 1986, only two had been introduced since 1941.

For the 135 years up to 1985 there were no arrivals at Kings Cross from Welwyn North between 0822 and 0835. In fact, the interval in the service at that time of day was never less than twenty minutes and sometimes much longer, being 39 minutes as recently as 1977. Despite a small trend towards an earlier start at work (*see* Chapter 14), this interval, in the middle of the peak period, remained at 24 minutes from 1982 to 1985. From 13 May 1985 an additional train was at last inserted. Departing Welwyn North at 0801 it ran non-stop to Finsbury Park, arriving at Kings Cross at 0825. Within days this train, re-timed to depart at 0805 in 1986, became Welwyn North's most used service. Popularly known as 'the Digswell Flyer' it occasionally overtook the 0750. The latter, re-timed to 0747 in 1986, had been added to the service in 1978. (*See* Figure 8.1.)

The introduction of the 0801 up service in 1985 (*see* Timetable Appendix B7) was part of a plan to increase the revenue-earning mileage of Class 313 units forming the only surviving southbound inner suburban semi-fast, the 0804 Welwyn Garden City to Kings Cross, and to relieve overcrowding on the 0737 fast from Royston. Neither of these trains served Welwyn North. The units forming the 0804 were re-rostered to provide an additional Welwyn Garden City to Kings Cross train an hour earlier, and the 0625 from Royston, which called at Welwyn North at 0656, was reduced from eight to four coaches. The four coaches removed from the latter were then used to form the 0801 which started from Stevenage at 0753, and stopped at Knebworth before running non-stop from Welwyn North to Finsbury Park.

In 1986 the 0801 was re-timed to depart from Welwyn North at 0805 and increased to eight coaches by the addition of four coaches from the 0842 which, since its deceleration in 1985, had become much less used. The 0805 was also re-diagrammed to start from Letchworth at 0746 and call at Hitchin at 0750.

There had been several earlier trains which ran from Welwyn North to Kings Cross with only one intermediate stop. The first,

introduced in 1906, ran non-stop to Finsbury Park after leaving Welwyn at 8.22 am, and continued to do so, after re-timing to 8.24 am in the mid 1920s, until 1939 in which year it started making an additional call at Welwyn Garden City. Nearly four decades had to pass before the next one-intermediate-stop train. This last was a slow train introduced in 1930, which was progressively accelerated, withdrawn in 1947, reinstated in 1966, and further accelerated in May 1977 to call at Welwyn Garden City before continuing non-stop to Kings Cross. This train, the 0718 departure from Welwyn North of May 1977, broke the 67-year-old 32-minute record from Welwyn North to Kings Cross by two minutes, but the service was withdrawn nine months later. Another train making only one intermediate stop was the 0834 which called at Finsbury Park only and ran for 4½ years from February 1978. This train was the result of various re-timings of the 8.22 am of 1906. In 1939 and 1982 additional calls were added and by 1986 the train had become the 0830 calling at Welwyn Garden City, Hatfield, Potters Bar and Finsbury Park. When running non-stop to Finsbury Park, it was timed so easily in some years that other trains with additional calls at Welwyn Garden City were actually faster.

The 0812 and 0856 departures from Welwyn North in 1986 originate from trains which have run without interruption since 1886 and 1870 respectively. From the mid 1950s to 1977 the 0812 was known affectionately as the 'Brookmans Park Flyer', as that was its last stop before Finsbury Park. Its arrival time in Kings Cross has always been between 0838 and 0848 and in 1986 was the same as in 1887, namely 0842. In 1984, when it was timed to depart from Welwyn North at 0814, about eighty passengers boarded it daily at Knebworth and 110 at Welwyn North. This was a very different situation from that of 1887 when it called at Knebworth on request only.

The 0856 departure, boarded by only about twenty-five passengers a day at Welwyn North in 1986, has been running since about 1870. At that time, when a later start at work was usual, it was a prime service, on which no delay could be permitted. Accordingly, horses were not conveyed on it. It remained unchanged from 1900 to 1938 during which period it departed Welwyn North at 0901, called at Hatfield and Finsbury Park, and terminated at Kings Cross at 0934.

With few exceptions, up passenger trains to London from Welwyn North terminated at Kings Cross. Occasional trains, such as those shown in Table 8.1 for 1884 and 1890, went to Moorgate, and for a short period in 1950/1 there was a direct train from Welwyn North (dep. 9.8 am) to Broad Street (arr. 9.49 am) calling only at Welwyn Garden City and Finsbury Park.

8.2   The down services

The longest tradition in the down (northbound) service is that of the 1708 (1986) from Kings Cross to Welwyn North. On the opening of the line in 1850, a 5 pm departure called at all stations to Hitchin; the intermediate stations to Welwyn at that time were Hornsey, Colney Hatch & Southgate (now New Southgate), Barnet (now New Barnet), Potter's Bar & South Mimms, and Hatfield for St Alban's and Luton. In 1858, the train (dep. 5.3 pm) ran non-stop to Hatfield, arriving at Welwyn in 36 minutes. This time was not equalled until 1887 and was beaten by only one minute by the fastest train of 1958. In 1862 the Hatfield stop was omitted unless a first class passenger from London required it, but the journey time to Welwyn, inclusive of new calls at Barnet and Potter's Bar, was 47 minutes. Horses and carriages were soon prohibited from being conveyed on this train, which in some timetables was shown as being divided at Hatfield, with the front portion running non-stop to Hitchin and the rear portion calling at all stations, including, of course, Welwyn.

From 1900 to the mid-1950s, the train always left Kings Cross at 5.10 pm and ran non-stop to Hatfield. Until the mid-1920s, despite the intervention of World War I, it always arrived at Hatfield at 5.34 pm and departed at 5.35 pm, calling at Welwyn at 5.42 pm. Its ultimate destination varied, including, for example, Cambridge, Hitchin and, improbably enough in the year 1910, Ashwell. In June 1965 this train was altered to terminate at Baldock instead of Royston.

Meanwhile, the Second World War failed to change the departure time of the 5.10 pm or its non-stop run to Hatfield, but since 1939 this train called additionally at Welwyn Garden City, and its arrival at Welwyn North was progressively retarded to 5.52 pm in 1941. A 1945 post-war acceleration was short-lived, the timing becoming progressively slower until December 1958 when it left Kings Cross at 5.12 pm and arrived at Welwyn North at 5.57 pm.

Dieselisation brought dramatic changes. In December 1959 the train, restored to a 5.10 pm departure, ran non-stop to Welwyn Garden City, reaching Welwyn North at 5.41 pm. By June 1970, a further acceleration brought the (then) 1717 into Welwyn North at 1746, a diesel timing as fast as any Kings Cross–Welwyn North electric train today, though with three fewer intermediate calls. In early 1977 this train was timetabled to depart from Kings Cross at its latest ever time of 1725, seventy minutes after the immediately preceding Kings Cross departure for Welwyn North. After that, until electrification, it departed at 1722 and ran non-stop to Welwyn North in 28 minutes.

With the advent of electrification its departure time has varied between 1707 and 1713 and its timing in 1979 was reduced to 26 minutes including calls at Finsbury Park and Welwyn Garden City. This equalled the previous fastest Kings Cross to Welwyn North service. Departing at 1708 in 1986, with the standard additional calls at Potters Bar and Hatfield, this train remains after 136 years one of Welwyn North's most important services.

The most popular train of all to Welwyn North, however, does not leave Kings Cross until over an hour later, at 1810. Conveying some ninety passengers to Welwyn North, this, of all northbound trains, has a good case for omitting some intermediate calls. It was introduced in 1967 with a departure time of 1804, and during 1971 and 1972 as a diesel-multiple-unit ran non-stop to Welwyn North in 26 minutes, a time which has never been bettered. This train replaced a 6 pm departure which had run fairly continuously since 1850, releasing a slip coach for Potters Bar in 1884, and dividing at Hatfield with fast and slow portions for Hitchin in 1890. It ceased to serve Welwyn North in 1942. Over the years numerous re-timings of the trains immediately before and after it resulted in an unacceptable interval in 1950 as already described. It was restored to Welwyn North as the 5.52 pm from Kings Cross shortly afterwards, becoming the fastest London to Welwyn North train at that time. A 1900 from Kings Cross which originated in 1884 became the well used 1840 which has served Welwyn North for its

Figure 8.1   *The up 0801 electric multiple unit (EMU) No 312/723 leaving Welwyn North station on the non-stop run to Finsbury Park on 15 July 1985*
                                                                    © *T. W. Gladwin*

whole career. This 1840 is the train, mentioned in Chapter 7, which is now assisted by two relief services.

The 1748 departure from Kings Cross of 1986 followed less than a quarter hour after the previous service to Welwyn North. Introduced in 1930 as the 5.34 pm from Kings Cross it has been variously retarded over the years. In 1967/8, by then re-timed to depart from Kings Cross at 1739, this train, which included a buffet car, ran non-stop to Welwyn North, as did the previous departure at 1714. Whilst much appreciated by travellers from London, this meant that there were no trains from Welwyn Garden City to Welwyn North between 1700 and 1830. The 1712, 1745 and 1811 down departures from Welwyn Garden City all ran non-stop from there to Knebworth.

The progressive re-timing of the 5.34 pm from Kings Cross eventually left such a large interval after the 1708 departure that a new train had to be inserted into the timetable. Introduced in 1976 as the 1727 from Kings Cross, it was re-timed to depart at 1734. In 1986 this train was allowed 33 minutes for the journey to Welwyn North, making it the slowest Monday-to-Saturday service between the two stations. However, being diagrammed to run slow-line to Welwyn Garden City, and further frequently delayed by traffic congestion due to the viaduct, it rarely ran to time. As a result Hertfordshire County Council made representations to British Railways about this less reliable service. None the less, as evident from Appendix C and Tables 8.1 and 8.2, the idea that the slowest train would one day take no more than 33 minutes would have been welcomed in 1958.

Chapter 9

Goods and Mineral

For the first seventy years of Great Northern Railway operations into London, the whole range of general goods traffic – coal, fish, meat and milk trains – passed through Welwyn. From a very modest beginning in 1851, when six or seven coal trains reached Kings Cross each week, this remunerative traffic increased by leaps and bounds, helped by the fact that sea-borne coal was selling in London at 30 shillings (£1.50) per ton but GNR coal was only 17 shillings (85p). By 1854 coal tonnage had increased to 281 559 tons per annum, mainly from Durham and South Yorkshire pits plus a small amount from Derbyshire. The tonnage had doubled by 1863 and in 1865 had reached no less than 975 000 tons per annum. Some of this increase was due to the opening of through communication from the GNR to the London, Chatham and Dover Railway via the Metropolitan Railway and Blackfriars. To eliminate the need for this cross London traffic to enter the Kings Cross goods yard, six sidings on either side of the main lines were installed at Hornsey in 1866. These were the genesis of the large Ferme Park yards that developed in later years.

Pending the extension of the Midland Railway from Bedford to London (St Pancras) that company's trains began working from Hitchin to Kings Cross in February 1858. This additional traffic placed a severe burden on GN line capacity south of Hitchin. On one day in November 1865 it was recorded that seventy-three GN goods and coal trains passed over the section as well as twenty-two Midland, about equally divided between up and down trains.

Only small 0-6-0 and 0-4-2 engines were available to haul the goods and coal trains and the returned empty wagons going back northwards. Usually loaded trains consisted of about thirty-five wagons. From 1865 the Locomotive Engineer, A. Sturrock, built a number of steam tenders for attachment to 0-6-0 engines with the idea that loads could be increased. These tenders had two cylinders supplied with exhaust steam from the engine. The idea was not a success and so Sturrock's successor, Patrick Stirling, dispensed with them. A contemporary observer on Welwyn station at three o'clock one morning, describes the passage of a coal train hauled by a steam tender engine, 'the syncopated beat of two separate sets of cylinders could be heard approaching. Exhaust steam from both engine and tender reflected an orange glow against the night sky as the fireman opened the firedoor to put in more coal. Over forty wagons rumbled by at 20 miles per hour'.

In 1888 the Ferme Park yards had become full-scale banks of sidings handling all the coal and returned-empty traffic, which by then had increased further by addition of more coal from Nottinghamshire and Derbyshire. Not until 1901 was any effort made to reduce the number of heavy goods and coal trains passing over the GN lines into London. The Midland trains had of course been using their own line from 1868 but the number of GN trains went on increasing.

Following the death of Patrick Stirling in 1895 his successor, H. A. Ivatt, faced a formidable task in providing more up-to-date locomotives to handle all classes of traffic. A start had to be made with passenger engines, followed in 1901 by a large 0-8-0 with 4' 8" driving wheels, capable of hauling up to sixty loaded wagons between Peterborough and Ferme Park. This enabled the number of trains to be reduced from forty-four to thirty-six each weekday. So the Ivatt 0-8-0 'Long Toms', as they were known, became an everyday sight at Welwyn. From 1907 until 1918 a number of them worked through from Nottingham (Colwick) to Ferme Park, returning next day with empty wagons. The crews had their regular booked engines on these duties on which they lodged overnight at Hornsey.

Coal trains from Colwick Sidings (Nottingham) and New England (Peterborough) were marshalled in the following four sections which indicate the large area to which coal passing through Welwyn was delivered:

(a) For the London, Brighton & South Coast Railway, London & South Western Railway, and the South East section of the South Eastern & Chatham Railway (SECR)

(b) For Hornsey, Brockley, Elephant & Castle (owned by the GNR), Crystal Palace, Nunhead, Clapham Road, Bricklayers Arms and stations on the London, Chatham and Dover section of the SECR (that is, Medway, Thames and Kent stations)

(c) For Hackney Wick, Poplar, East India Dock, High Barnet and Edgware branches, Ashburton Grove, Highbury Vale, Clarence Yard, Kings Cross, Finsbury Park and Caledonian Road

(d) For Kings Cross (loco) only on certain trains from Peterborough.

The next development commenced in 1913 when H. N. Gresley brought out the first of a 2-cylinder heavy mineral design 2-8-0 (Class O1), also with 4' 8" wheels, capable of hauling up to eighty loaded coal wagons for a total weight of around 1350 tons. Wartime restrictions delayed production of this type which was soon joined by a 3-cylinder version (Class O2). Most of these two classes operated the heaviest coal, general goods and brick trains from Peterborough to London down to 1932. In 1927 most of the Ivatt 0-8-0s had moved away and the total number of trains into London had been reduced still further; nine coal, eight goods and five brick trains passed through Welwyn towards London and in the northbound direction there were thirty-one goods and empty wagon trains. One of the up coal trains at this time, the 9.25 am New England to Ferme Park was hauled by one of the new Gresley Class P1 5' 2" 2-8-2 'Mikado' engines, loaded to one hundred wagons. This train was due through Welwyn at 1.55 pm and the return trip with a hundred empty wagons started from Ferme Park at 5.35

am and so was not usually seen by railway enthusiasts. With the introduction of automatic colour-light signals at certain points in 1934–5, these one hundred wagon trains were too long for the sections and were discontinued. Thereafter the trains worked by these 'Mikado' locomotives were normally of eighty but sometimes up to ninety-two wagons.

A fresh development came in 1932 when two weekday fast coal trains limited to fifty-six loaded wagons commenced to run from Peterborough to Ferme Park. These trains had a loaded 5-ton brick wagon next to the Class K3 2-6-0 engine to give extra braking power as these wagons were vacuum-braked. Total running time was reduced to around 3¾ hours compared with up to 8 hours for the eighty wagon trains. Both engines and crews of the fast trains were turned round quickly at Hornsey and returned to Peterborough with empty wagon trains, thus making single-shift working a reality. This experiment reduced line occupation and manpower costs but was not developed for another decade.

Over the ten years 1925–35 the Gresley 2-8-0s of both two- and three-cylinder varieties (Classes O1 and O2), together with the two P1 2-8-2s continued to handle the coal trains between Peterborough and Hornsey. They were assisted by some ex Great Central Railway (GCR) Class O4 2-8-0s of Robinson's well known design, which tended to haul the lighter goods trains. These latter were replaced by additional K3 2-6-0s in 1935. The next major change came in 1943 when 35 new Ministry of Supply 'Austerity' 2-8-0s were allocated on loan to New England shed and immediately commenced work on the coal trains to Ferme Park. Eventually eight Class A coal trains were operated each weekday to timings around three hours with sixty wagons. A similar number of empty wagon trains made up to seventy wagons worked northbound, making it possible for both New England and Hornsey crews to work out and home duties. A smaller number of these trains was also booked on Sundays. Towards the end of 1944 the 'Austerities' were required for overseas service with the War Department and the LNER had to revert to their previous arrangements for coal train haulage.

Figure 9.1   *BR Cl. 9F 2–10–0 No 92188 on a train of empty coal wagons emerging from Welwyn South Tunnel on 1 June 1963*   © *G. W. Goslin*

Following the cessation of hostilities the War Department began returning their engines to Britain and the LNER purchased some two hundred and classed them O7. Some were again allocated to the New England–Ferme Park services, most of which were upgraded to Class A, with overall timings averaging 3 hours 50 minutes, including a stop at Hitchin for water. The return empties were allowed 3¼ hours on average. This situation continued until 1954 when some British Railways Standard Cl. 9F 2-10-0 engines arrived at New England to replace the 'Austerities' on the coal trains. In April 1963 when sufficient 2750 hp Type 4 Brush diesels became available a scheme of seven loaded coal trains was put into operation. On these duties ninety loaded wagons of 1540 gross tons were hauled at average speeds of 35 mph. This enabled reductions to be made in the total trains needed of six up loaded and four down empties. A

little over three years later, in August 1966, it was decided to discontinue all the coal haulage from Peterborough to Ferme Park and to close the yards at the latter place. Thus, after more than a century, coal trains ceased passing through Welwyn.

In addition to the coal traffic there was a considerable amount of general merchandise conveyed by slow moving trains, such as iron and steel products from the north east and machinery from various points such as Stamford and Grantham. Less well known were the two Monday-to-Friday potato trains from Lincolnshire, which were hauled by Gresley 2-8-0 engines and passed through Welwyn in the late evening. Between them they carried some 2000 tons of Lincolnshire potatoes for the London markets. More important was the large number of bi-directional fast-braked goods services. The down trains mostly left Kings Cross goods station in the late afternoon and evening hours. From a humble beginning in 1895 the GNR developed a substantial traffic to many distant places, some in direct competition with the rival Midland and LNWR Companies. This was particularly the case with Manchester and Liverpool to which cities the GNR ran trains over a period of some forty years. In

Figure 9.2   *LNER Class V2 2–6–2 No 60911 on the down Scotch goods between the tunnels in 1953*   © *G. W. Goslin*

1927, for example, ten such northbound braked goods trains passed through Welwyn daily. These included the famous Glasgow Goods which started out at 3.40 pm until its later years when it was brought forward to 3.5 pm. This train was initially lightly loaded to thirty-two wagons and a bogie brake vehicle and hauled by passenger engines. In 1913 new Gresley 2-6-0s became responsible for the duty and in 1921 they were themselves succeeded by the larger K3 2-6-0s which hauled fifty wagon trains until 1936. In turn these were replaced by Gresley's Class V2 'Green Arrow' 2-6-2s. (*See* Figure 9.2.) Much later in the 1950s this duty was considered of such importance that it was afforded Pacific haulage throughout from London to Newcastle with Top Link crews and thereby maintained a good standard of punctuality. In addition to the above mentioned goods services there were through trains to Grimsby, Nottingham, the West Riding and York.

Similar services operated in the reverse direction, most of which passed through Welwyn in the night hours. In addition there were fish trains, two each from Hull and Grimsby and one from Aberdeen passing through Welwyn between 9 pm and 2.30 am Mondays to Fridays, and two express milk trains, the 5.40 pm from Stafford and 10.15 pm from Egginton, which passed at midnight and 2.30 am respectively. These conveyed milk in churns or glass lined tanks from the farms in Staffordshire and Derbyshire to London and were mostly unloaded at Finsbury Park or Kings Cross with some going forward to Finchley by local services. This traffic started in the 1880s and did not cease until 1950. Empty milk churns and tanks returned northwards through Welwyn in special trains at 8 am and 4 pm weekdays and 9 am Sundays. Likewise empty fish vans went down in mid-mornings to Hull, Doncaster and Grimsby.

It remains to describe the local goods trains which called at Welwyn to leave and collect such traffic as was on offer there. In the early LNER period, northbound services began with the 3.40 am Ferme Park to Sandy manure train conveying wagon loads of stable manure, and some from the London Zoo, to wayside stations. This called at Welwyn at about 4.50 am to set down wagons when required and was quickly followed by the 3 am Kings Cross goods to Peterborough which set down wagons of goods at Welwyn at 5.10 am. However the real shunting and pick-up work was done by train No 317 down 9 am Ferme Park to Peterborough, which spent ten minutes (11.35 to 11.45 am) at Welwyn to pick up loaded wagons for northbound destinations. By 1935 the originating point of this train had become Ashburton Grove, where it collected wagons of household refuse to set down at Hatfield for onward conveyance to tips on the branch lines. It was at Welwyn North from 11.20 to 11.50 am. No other northbound goods trains called there. In 1947 this train had become No 1122 down which spent only thirteen minutes at Welwyn North from 10.10 to 10.23 am. Southbound, the 7.20 am Peterborough to Ferme Park stopped at Welwyn North from 1.55 to 2.5 pm to set down coal and the 9.35 am from Peterborough set down cattle only when required at 2 pm. Finally No 305, 7.15 am from Peterborough, which undertook all the pick-up work as far south as New Barnet, took no less than 10½ hours to complete its journey. It set down goods and coal at Welwyn North and attached loaded wagons, also between 2.5 and 2.15 pm. Tranship vans were collected by No 381 up 10.30 am Peterborough to Ferme Park, stopping from 1.24 to 1.35 pm for only one shunting movement. No 345, the 9.50 am up coal from New England, also called to detach coal wagons at 2.20 pm. All these trains would be worked at various times by 0-6-0, 2-8-0 or in early days by 0-8-0 locomotives. By 1947 there were only two up goods calling at Welwyn North, No 1111, the 7.40 am up Hitchin to Ferme Park, which took up tranships in one shunt between 10.50 and 10.59 am, and No 1123 up, which afforded a later service for wagon loads. This started from New England at 7.15 am and stopped at Welwyn North from 3.30 to 3.45 pm.

Over the years Welwyn usually had a shunt horse which was used to deliver local goods on a flat platform dray and to shunt wagons in both up and down yards, transferring them from one to the other when required. The last horse at Welwyn North was Tom, who was finally retired in 1947 or 1948.

Figure 9.3 *Tom the Welwyn North shunting horse with his driver Charles Halls, 1938*
© R. Temple

wagons attached to stopping goods trains and intended for consigning goods between intermediate stations. These vans were operated on regular trains, Welwyn North being covered in the up direction by the 8.10 pm from Hitchin to Hornsey (10.35 am from Peterborough), which picked up tranships at Welwyn North between 11 and 11.15 pm. Train No 317 (11.20 am Hatfield to Hitchin) called at Welwyn North at 11.35 am and the 2.10 am Clarence Yard (Finsbury Park) to Hitchin (meat vans) served Welwyn North.

Although normally sent by passenger train, an important traffic from Welwyn North was the despatch of cases of live bees from the well known firm E. H. Taylor & Co., successors to the original owner Thomas B. Blow (*c*.1885) whose premises were purposely situated close to the station to speed the delivery of goods. The firm closed in 1984 and the site was re-occupied for light industrial purposes.

With the introduction of Class 317 units (May 1986) bicycles ceased to be accepted on trains from Welwyn North because of the need to reserve the lockable compartment for parcels or mails. A concession was, however, subsequently made to carry bicycles at weekends.

Inevitably changes took place over the years. By 1932 the down manure train had been discontinued because of reduced traffic due to replacement of horse-drawn carts by motor vehicles. Post-war changes were rapid as the transfer of traffic from rail to road made for less use of local stations. At Welwyn North the local goods trains remained the same, apart from small changes in times, until in 1957–8 both Nos 1122 down and 1123 up were calling only if required. The official closure date for Welwyn North goods yards was 26 November 1967.

Another less well known train calling at Welwyn North from the 1930s was the 2.40 am Sundays Kings Cross to Peterborough newspapers which stopped at 3.21 am. After the war this train was extended to Boston and conveyed forces personnel to Peterborough, Spalding and Boston. It was, in its later years, worked by a Boston B1 4-6-0 and crew who had worked up on a fish train from Grimsby on Saturday night.

It is not widely known that the pick-up goods trains also provided a service for the conveyance of small consignments. For this purpose the LNER operated road vans or tranships for a number of years from 1927. These were in fact covered goods

Figure 9.4 *BR Cl. 31 diesel-electric locomotive No 31171 on a down train of nine grain wagons approaching Welwyn North station on 15 July 1985* © T. W. Gladwin

Chapter 10

Motive Power

Early locomotives used on trains passing Welwyn were 'Little Sharps' having 2-2-2 wheel arrangement and weighing about 18½ tons and 'Small Hawthorns', also 2-2-2s, but heavier at 27 tons, all being to the makers' standard designs.

In 1851 the new Locomotive Engineer, A. Sturrock, who had previously worked at Swindon, on the Great Western Railway, introduced 2-4-0 type locomotives weighing 28 tons. Next came ten engines built to Crampton's Patent design with a curious 4-2-0 wheel arrangement, soon altered to 2-2-2. Goods traffic was hauled by small 0-4-2 and 0-6-0 engines of various makers' designs. Some of the 0-6-0s were coupled to steam tenders having an auxiliary 2-cylinder engine, taking exhaust steam from the boiler. These, however, were not entirely successful and were not long in service.

In 1866 the legendary Patrick Stirling was appointed Locomotive Engineer. His first designs were 2-4-0s of 34½ tons, followed by larger 0-6-0s for goods and coal traffic and later by some 0-4-2 locomotives for mixed traffic work. Being a firm believer in the value of a single pair of driving wheels for express passenger duties, Stirling built at Doncaster some 2-2-2 engines with 7' 1" driving wheels. In 1870 came the first of fifty-three 'Singles' with 8' 1" driving wheels and outside cylinders, straightback (domeless) boilers and a leading bogie making the type 4-2-2. The first engine carried the number 1. Many express trains through Welwyn were hauled by this famous class which gave the GNR supremacy in fast schedules for many years. No 1 was eventually preserved and housed in the Railway Museum at York whence in 1938 it was put into running order to work a special train of vintage rolling stock (*see* Chapter 11) from Kings Cross to Stevenage on 30 June in connection with publicising a new train set for the 'Flying Scotsman'. This unique event stirred the imagination of railway enthusiasts who turned out in large numbers to see the veteran in action.

A far better opportunity came on 11 September 1938 when the Railway Correspondence and Travel Society ran a special charter for their members and guests over the 76¼ miles from Kings Cross to Peterborough and return. It was an outstanding success, watched by untold numbers of the public from lineside vantage points. In more recent times No 1 has again emerged from retirement to run on certain preserved railways and is now housed in the National Railway Museum at York.

The services to Welwyn have always been closely associated with those from Kings Cross to Cambridge and in earlier days

Figure 10.1 *GNR Stirling 8 feet 'Single' 4–2–2 No 1 on the down RCTS special train from Kings Cross to Peterborough on 11 September 1938, between Sandy and Tempsford* *Courtesy of D. E. White*

a large proportion of these trains stopped at Welwyn *en route*. It is of interest to note the motive power allocated to these trains up to 1922. From 1880 to 1890 Archibald Sturrock's 2-4-0s Nos 229 and 240 as rebuilt by Patrick Stirling were used, together with Stirling's 2-2-2s Nos 21, 41 and 61 (built in 1868). The next decade saw the introduction of Stirling's 2-4-0s Nos 867 and 872. From 1902 onwards H. A. Ivatt's locomotives predominated, firstly with his GNR Class E1 2-4-0s Nos 206, 751, 1061–4 and 1066–70, and then with his well known 4-4-0s GNR Class D1 Nos 49, 1388/9 and D2 1072/7/8/9. After 1918 came his well known 'Klondyke' 4-4-2 Atlantics, Nos 252/3/4 and 949 and the large Atlantics Nos 1400 and 1426. In the immediate pre-grouping period, 1920–2, Ivatt's Superheated Class D1 4-4-0s Nos 59–62 were introduced to the services.

The Cambridge line from Kings Cross has from 1924 onwards had an association with royal trains as this was the route royalty took when travelling to Sandringham. Great Eastern Railway (GER) based locomotives were normally used, as for example, its Claud Hamilton 4-4-0 as LNER No 1872E pulled the royal train from Wolferton to Kings Cross on 3 November 1924 and LNER No 8848 of the same class, on Queen Alexandra's funeral train to Kings Cross on 16 November 1925.

Other references to royal engines seen at Welwyn in more recent times are given later in this chapter.

On the death of Stirling in 1895 the time had come for the GNR to have more powerful express locomotives. The new engineer, H. A. Ivatt, designed the first British 'Atlantic' (4-4-2) engine No 990, *Henry Oakley*, the only named engine on the GNR until 1922. Twenty-two of this class were built and they were followed by a larger version from 1902, the Ivatt Atlantics with unprecedentedly large boilers 5' 6" in. diameter. Eventually ninety-four of these were built and they ran all the expresses down to 1922, being gradually relegated to secondary trains and peak-period reliefs as more 'Pacific' 4-6-2s entered service. Even so they were called upon in emergencies and did good work during the Second World War.

By the turn of the century coal traffic into London had grown so much that there was a demand for more powerful engines than 0-6-0s hauling only about forty wagons. So Ivatt designed an 0-8-0 capable of hauling sixty loaded coal wagons, thus reducing the number of trains required.

Ivatt retired in 1911 and was succeeded by H. N. Gresley who had trained at Crewe and Horwich on the LNWR and Lancashire & Yorkshire Railway, and had been the GNR Carriage and Wagon Superintendent. Gresley's first task was to build up the mixed traffic and heavy coal-train locomotive stock. In 1913 came the first GNR 2-6-0 mixed-traffic class, seen through Welwyn on both semi-fast and stopping passenger trains as well as on fast goods. These were followed by a large Class O1 2-8-0 for mineral trains, capable of pulling eighty loaded wagons. Both were 2-cylinder designs, which after the First World War were supplemented by new 3-cylinder designs incorporating the well-known Gresley derived motion.

An entirely new development came in the spring of 1922 when the first of Gresley's 3-cylinder Pacific (4-6-2) express passenger engines was turned out of Doncaster Works. These well proportioned and handsome looking locomotives were adopted by the LNER as a standard class and eventually totalled seventy-nine, mostly carrying names of famous race horses.

Apart from those coming from other lines in the Eastern group, locomotives from other railways which passed through Welwyn were few. Soon after the 1923 grouping the railways were in competition to claim the 'best' locomotive, and following the British Empire Exhibition at Wembley in 1924 where LNER *Flying Scotsman* and GWR *Caerphilly Castle* were displayed, an historic exchange of locomotives was made between the two railway companies. The Great Western provided 4-6-0 'Castle' Class No 4079 *Pendennis Castle* in exchange for LNER Pacific 4-6-2 No 4474 later named *Victor Wild*. The trials lasted for two weeks in April/May 1925, the GWR locomotive on alternate days working the 10.10 am from Kings Cross to Leeds as far as Grantham, returning at 3.7 pm, and the 1.30 pm from Kings Cross to Leeds as far as Doncaster, returning at 6.21 pm.

In 1925 two more powerful mineral locomotives were introduced to speed up the coal trains between Peterborough and Ferme Park, Hornsey, so as to minimise track occupation along this busy section. They were Class P1 'Mikado' 2-8-2s Nos 2393 and 2394 and with their large 'Pacific' boilers made an impressive sight on the viaduct with their 100-wagon trains. Both locomotives were withdrawn in 1945, being superseded by the 2-8-0 Austerity locomotives which became surplus to War Department use and continued until the end of steam haulage.

For the streamlined trains introduced between 1935 and 1937 an improved Pacific design emerged. The first of these, fully streamlined and painted in silver grey, was named *Silver Link*. On its first public trip from Kings Cross down to Barkston Junction near Grantham, history was made. Having topped the long rise to Potters Bar at an unprecedented 75 mph and reaching 95 mph through Hatfield, it passed Welwyn North at an unusual 88 mph. Then just after Stevenage, it attained the magic 100 mph. It sustained this for the twenty-five miles down to Offord and reached a maximum of 112½ mph at Arlesey. Three days later *Silver Link* went into regular service on the new 'Silver Jubilee' express which was an outstanding commercial success. Eventually the Class A4 Pacifics reached a total of thirty-five, of which four carried names with a 'Silver' element for working the 'Silver Jubilee', five were named after British Commonwealth countries and painted in garter-blue livery for use on the 'Coronation' express in 1937 and two, for the 'West Riding Limited', were named *Golden Fleece* and *Golden Shuttle*. (*See* Figure 6.4.) Others carried bird names of which the most famous was *Mallard* because on 7 July 1938 it achieved a world record maximum speed of 126 mph in the course of a special trial run.

Meantime, Gresley had produced his deservedly famous mixed traffic 2-6-2 'Green Arrow' Class V2 used on both passenger and fast goods work, which was particularly useful in the wartime years.

After Gresley died in 1941 his successors built more Pacifics to four differing designs which, together with the Gresley engines, worked the East Coast route until the advent of dieselisation, fully implemented from 1963.

The outer suburban trains down to the outbreak of the Second World War were worked by GNR Ivatt 4-4-0s, small and large Atlantics and, from 1928 a few ex-GCR 4-6-2T of Class A5 appeared on the Baldock trains. By the end of the war both Ivatt 4-4-0s and Atlantics were worn out and were replaced from 1946 by new 4-6-0s of Class B1 designed by E. Thompson and from 1948 by new Class L1 Thompson 2-6-4Ts.

Over the years from 1932 to 1939 and 1948 to 1960 the fast 'Cambridge Buffet Expresses' were hauled by Ivatt Atlantics, large and small, ex-GER Claud Hamilton 4-4-0s and B12 and B17 4-6-0s, also for a time by one GCR 4-4-2, No 6083. Between 1948 and 1960 Class B1 4-6-0s and Class L1 2-6-4Ts were also used, the latter only occasionally. One of the most notable locomotive workings from Cambridge shed was undertaken by two specially painted and embellished Class D16 Super Claud 4-4-0s Nos 8783 and 8787. These were kept in prime condition for use on royal trains between Kings Cross and Wolferton (Norfolk) which they hauled between London and Kings Lynn, from where other specially kept engines covered the short run

Figure 10.2   *LNER Class L1 2–6–4T No 67746 on an up 'Cambridge Buffet Express' passing Welwyn North station on 3 August 1957*   © *H. J. Stull*

to Wolferton. Until September 1939 in normal service either Nos 8783 or 8787 worked the stopping train that left Cambridge about 1.55 pm, and passed Welwyn North shortly before 3 pm, and returning from London at 6.55 pm, stopped at Welwyn North at various times between 7.40 and 7.50 pm. A fresh royal engine was allocated to Cambridge in 1946. This was Class B2 4-6-0 No 1671 *Royal Sovereign*. Like its predecessors it was always kept in impeccable condition and its normal regular duties also included an afternoon train from Cambridge to Kings Cross, returning in the evening. Other engines seen on Cambridge trains were B17 'Sandringham' 4-6-0s, some of which were named after football clubs and had a miniature ball on one splasher with the club colours beneath. (*See* Figure 11.3.)

A Daimler-engined petrol driven rail car was delivered by the makers, Dick, Kerr & Co, to the GNR at Doncaster in September 1904, running under its own power the 156 miles to London, prior to experimental use on the Hatfield to Hertford branch early the following year.

Mention must be made of an unusual type of train which, used elsewhere on weekdays, served Welwyn on Sundays only for a number of years down to 1914; it consisted of a single coach Ivatt steam motor car propelled by a small integral 0-4-0 engine. Seating was provided for ten first and thirty-six third class passengers. This unit left Hitchin at 9.30 am and 2.5 pm and Knebworth at 4.5 pm for Hatfield. It stopped at Welwyn at 9.59 am, 2.33 pm and 4.14 pm and returning at 12.43 pm, 3.1 pm and 4.46 pm, the 3.1 going only to Knebworth. Connections to and from London were made at Hatfield.

In 1910 the motor car was timed stopping at all stations Hatfield to Hitchin it took 39 minutes, compared with 28 minutes for a conventional train. In 1986, with one more station, Welwyn Garden City, the timing was 22 minutes by electric trains.

On 29 May 1924 two GNR steam rail cars Nos 5 and 6, coupled back to back, ran empty to Hitchin via Welwyn prior to entering service on the Hitchin to Hertford line in June.

During the Second World War motive power workings gradu-

Figure 10.3   *King George V's funeral train hauled by LNER 'Sandringham' Class 4–6–0 No 2847* Helmingham Hall *from Kings Lynn to Kings Cross, passing Welwyn Garden City station on 23 January 1936*
Courtesy of Welwyn Garden City Library

ally became totally unpredictable, with most trains having a wide variety of power rather than the regular types as in pre-war times. Main line work was mostly in the hands of Gresley Pacifics Classes A1/3/4 and the versatile mixed-traffic V2 2-6-2s. Outer suburban work serving Welwyn North remained in the hands of the aged Ivatt 4-4-2 Atlantics with assistance at times from B17 'Sandringham' 4-6-0s from Cambridge, together with former Great Eastern types of 4-4-0 and 4-6-0.

In April 1941 the sudden death of Sir Nigel Gresley foreshadowed changes in policy which did not in fact come until two years later, beginning in March 1943 when the first rebuild of the six unique Class P2 2-8-2 'Cock o' the North' express locomotives passed through Welwyn North on its first trip to London following rebuilding as a Class A2/2 4-6-2. The most notable change came in April 1943 when a number of Ministry of Supply Austerity 2-8-0 locomotives were loaned to the LNER pending their shipment to Europe in 1944. These began work

Plate 6   *BR InterCity 125 High Speed Train (HST) between the Welwyn tunnels on*
17 July 1986   © *T. W. Gladwin*

on the increased number of heavy coal trains between Peterborough and Hornsey, making it possible to organise eight weekday fast coal and return-empty trains. When these engines were returned to the War Department for shipment abroad, the coal trains reverted to their former power of Gresley 2-8-0 and 2-6-0 classes until the Austerities returned in 1945 and 1946. There was also a short lived use of some Austerity 2-10-0 locomotives. Some residents of Welwyn would have been surprised to note a former GCR Class B2 4-6-0 No 5425 *City of Manchester* hauling the 5.55 pm from Kings Cross passenger train one night in April 1944.

Shortly after this the first Class B1 4-6-0 No 8301 *Springbok*, built to the design of the new CME Edward Thompson, was working on Kings Cross to Cambridge stopping trains as well as to Peterborough. This was followed in September by No 8304 *Gazelle* running regularly from Cambridge and used once on the royal train. The early period of E. Thompson's tenure at Doncaster Works was notable for the number of experimental rebuilds of existing Gresley classes. Examples of these were seen on the GN lines into London during 1945, such as A2/2 No 2003 *Lord President* (formerly P2), A2/1 No 3697 (modified V2), A1 No 4470 *Great Northern* (the pioneer Gresley Pacific) and B2 No 2871 *Manchester City*. In the next year, 1946, the last of these four was renamed to become the *Royal Sovereign* already mentioned, which was designated for use on royal trains between London and Kings Lynn, and thus appeared on the slow Cambridge trains calling at Welwyn North. In the spring of that year the first Thompson standard Pacific, with 6' 2" diameter driving wheels, Class A2 (later A2/3), appeared in the shape of No 500 *Edward Thompson*, and was later followed by four more for use in the southern area of the LNER. This locomotive had the distinction of being named after its designer whilst he was still in office.

By the end of the war the majority of the Ivatt Atlantics were forty or more years old and those stationed in the London District had become very run-down through lack of proper maintenance or spare parts. Because many were laid up awaiting repair there was a shortage of power for Hitchin and Cambridge stopping trains; those still working often caused delay through failure or just poor performance, inadequate even for the leisurely timetable then in force. The situation caused severe problems to the operators and many complaints from passengers.

Unusual locomotives, such as K3 2-6-0, V2 2-6-2, J39 0-6-0, N2 0-6-2T (from Hitchin shed), D9 4-4-0 (ex-GCR) and even a 48-year-old Ivatt 4-4-0 No 4309, its normal duties on permanent-way department trains, were pressed into service on passenger trains. The situation began to improve early in 1947 by which time Hitchin shed had received fourteen new Class B1 4-6-0s and Kings Cross had begun to use its quota of nine. Further improvements in outer suburban services came late in 1948 with the arrival of six Thompson Class L1 2-6-4T locomotives at Hitchin. These were successful on the stopping trains but less so on the faster duties on which it was often difficult for the firemen to maintain enough steam, and the locomotives had a startling propensity to fracture their connecting rods. The small diameter (5' 2") of their driving wheels made their coupling rods move very fast at high speeds, producing a noise which led to their being referred to as 'concrete mixers'.

By far the most interesting events of 1948 were occasioned by the interchange trials between locomotives from each of the four groups working over each of the four new British Rail regions. On the Eastern Region trials were run between Kings Cross and Leeds with the 1.10 pm down and 7.50 am from Leeds next day. Former LMS locomotives Royal Scot Class 4-6-0 No 46162 *Queens Westminster Rifleman* and Coronation Class 4-6-2 No 46236 *City of Bradford* were followed by ex-GWR King Class No 6018 *King Henry VI* and ex-SR Merchant Navy 4-6-2 No 35017 *Belgian Marine*. These unique trials were closely followed by lineside observers. Trials were also conducted with heavy goods locomotives between Peterborough and Hornsey using Austerity 2-10-0 No 73774 and 2-8-0 No 63169, ex-LNER 2-8-0 No 63773, ex-LMS 2-8-0 No 48189 and ex-GWR 2-8-0 No 3803.

New main line locomotive types came out in 1948 beginning with No E530 *Sayajirao*, a Pacific incorporating the new CME, A. H. Peppercorn's amendments to the Thompson design of 1946/7 and a completely new Pacific with 6' 8" driving wheels Class A1 No 60114 *W. P. Allen*.

In 1948 too, the 'Cambridge Buffet Express' services were resumed on timings around ten minutes longer than pre-war. Cambridge shed used B1 and B17 4-6-0s and sometimes B2 No 61671 on these trains, while Kings Cross and Hitchin normally provided B1 or very occasionally L1 locomotives. In January 1936 a Class B17 4-6-0, No 2847 *Helmingham Hall*, was used from Kings Lynn to Kings Cross on the funeral train of King George V (*see* Figure 10.3); when King George VI died in February 1952 British Railways Standard Pacific No 70000 *Britannia* was used for a similar duty.

Between 1951 and 1955 examples of the London Midland

Figure 10.4　LMS Cl. 4 2–6–4T No 42374 leaving Welwyn North station on a stopping train to Kings Cross on 26 September 1956. The train consists of 'bogie local' (Quad-art) suburban coaches　　　　　　　© *H. J. Stull*

Region Cl 4 2-6-0s were to be seen at Welwyn. Their somewhat unattractive appearance caused them to be known as 'Clodhoppers'. On 14 July 1948 No 43018 underwent suitability trials on a Kings Cross to Peterborough No 1 braked goods train and on 4 August 1951 No 43080 hauled a Peterborough to Kings Cross slow passenger train. No 43146 went south to Hornsey on 29 April 1954.

In the 1951 winter timetable travellers to Welwyn North were able to avail themselves of a faster return journey from London each evening by the 5.52 pm Cambridge and Peterborough train which called only at Finsbury Park and then Welwyn North. At first it was hauled by two locomotives, a Peterborough A2/3, often No 60533 *Happy Knight*, and a Kings Cross B1.

From time to time British Rail standard locomotives were seen at Welwyn, doubtless to assess their capabilities on this line. To cite a few examples, a Cl. 4 2-6-0 No 76035 spent a few weeks in the spring of 1955 working Kings Cross to Cambridge passenger trains and night freight trains to Hull; from late 1957 Cl. 5 4-6-0s Nos 73157 and 73158 were used, the former on Cambridge passenger trains, which on one occasion became stuck in a snowdrift between Ashwell and Royston. They too worked to Hull on freight trains, and 73158 on a Newmarket Race special; they left the area in October 1958. Then, due to an acute shortage of locomotives at Kings Cross, Standard Class 4 2-6-4Ts Nos 80103 and 80137 were obtained on loan for two weeks in September 1958 and worked outer suburban trains and empty stock workings into and out of Kings Cross. During the same year, two former GCR 4-6-2Ts, LNER Class A5 Nos 69814 and 69824, were borrowed for these duties. Another feature of the 1958 scene was the use by Cambridge of the LNER Class K1 2-6-0s on the Cambridge to Kings Cross service, examples being No 62019 on the 4.15 pm to Kings Cross on 15 and 16 August and No 62066 on the same train on 20 December.

British Railways Standard Cl. 9F 2-10-0 locomotives began to work the Peterborough to Hornsey coal trains in late 1954 and in the following years were occasionally pressed into service on summer relief passenger expresses. A fine sight on the viaduct on 5 August 1958 was one of these locomotives on a 24-coach empty stock train, bringing three sets of 8-car articulated inner suburban coaches back to London after their use on Nottingham to Skegness excursions.

British Railways Standard Britannia Pacifics were seen regularly from 1961 working the Cleethorpes to London expresses following their transfer from the GE Section where they had been replaced by diesel locomotives.

More 'foreign' locomotives were seen through Welwyn in the 1950s and 1960s, principally on railway enthusiast specials or charter trains. But there were two important exceptions.

In January 1955 two LMS Cl 4 2-6-4Ts, Nos 42328 and 42374, arrived at Hitchin for use on outer suburban trains. At first they hauled the 5.10 am Kings Cross to Baldock parcel trains, perhaps as a form of crew training. Later they were seen on the Kings Cross to Hitchin services and on empty coaching stock duties to and from Kings Cross. It would appear they were none too successful on this line and were transferred to Gorton (Manchester) in May 1957. (*See* Figure 10.4.)

In February 1956, two locomotives equipped with automatic warning systems in the drivers' cabs were borrowed from Crewe. They were to test the installation of apparatus sited on the track, between the rails, which gave an audible warning in the cab of the position of the signals ahead. On the 16th of the month ex-LMS Cl. 5 4-6-0 No 44911 worked the down 2.5 pm 'Cambridge Buffet Express' from Kings Cross, returning the next day with the 6.21 pm from Cambridge. This locomotive had worked through Welwyn on a diverted goods train from the LMR following the derailment of the up 'Royal Scot' at Watford on 3 February 1954. The other locomotive, British Railways Cl. 5 4-6-0 No 73071 worked the 6.5 am slow passenger train from Kings Cross to Cambridge on 17 February. The tests continued for some months before the locomotives were returned to their home region.

Coinciding with the gradual demise of steam haulage the railway enthusiast specials became something of a spectacle as they sped over Digswell Viaduct. What a sight was GW City

Class 4-4-0 No 3440 *City of Truro* (of the claimed speed record of 102.3 mph in 1904) piloting the crimson-lake Midland Compound 4-4-0 No 1000, on the special train from Kings Cross to Doncaster on 20 April 1960. Unhappily *City of Truro* had to be detached south of Peterborough on the return trip on account of a hot axle box. And just six days later the Compound 4-4-0 was coupled to former LNER Class B12/3 4-6-0 No 61572 on a similar trip to Doncaster. In 1963 LMS locomotives were to be seen on special trains between Kings Cross and the North. On 9 June 'Coronation' Pacific 4-6-2 No 46245 *City of London* worked a special train from Kings Cross to Doncaster and back whilst on the previous day LMS 'Jubilee' 4-6-0 No 45597 *Barbados* arrived at Kings Cross on a charter train from Bradford. The Great Western was again represented on 17 September and 8 October 1967 when 'Castle' 4-6-0 7029 *Clun Castle* (*see* Figure 10.6)

Figure 10.5   *LMS Cl. 5 4–6–0 No 44911 on the 8.10 am Kings Cross to Cambridge train approaching New Barnet station during 1956. Note the BR non-corridor coaches*
© *J. F. Aylard*

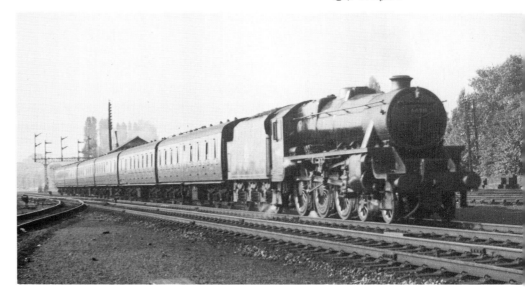

Figure 10.6   GWR 'Castle' Class 4–6–0 No 7029 Clun Castle *approaching Welwyn North station on a Rail Enthusiasts special train from Kings Cross to Leeds on 17 September 1967*
© G. W. Goslin

worked enthusiast specials from Kings Cross to Leeds and York respectively, well after steam-haulage of scheduled services had ceased. A less spectacular appearance occurred on 20 October 1966 when Southern 'Merchant Navy' 4-6-2 No 35026 *Lamport and Holt Line* passed over the viaduct light engine *en route* from the SR to York to work a special on from there to Newcastle. 35026 returned light engine to the SR on 22 October.

It had been officially envisaged that steam haulage of all trains south of Peterborough would cease with the commencement of the summer timetable on 17 June 1963, but because of shortages and failures of the replacement diesel locomotives, steam continued to make its appearance frequently; up to 20 April 1964 no fewer than 243 steam locomotive workings to Kings Cross or Hornsey were noted. By May 1964, apart from the special trains listed in Table 10.1, and possibly other unrecorded workings, the steam locomotive had vanished from the Welwyn scene for ever.

As far as can be ascertained the last steam-hauled scheduled train to Kings Cross was the up 'Tees–Tyne Pullman' from Newcastle on 20 April 1964 with Class A1 4-6-2 No 60114 *W. P. Allen* at its head. By some quirk of circumstance Class A3 4-6-2 No 60112 *St Simon* managed to penetrate the defences at Peterborough on 11 November 1964 with a train of empty coaches which were detached at Enfield. 60112 probably returned north light engine via Hornsey and the main line through Welwyn.

It is appropriate to recall that the final run of the famous 4472 *Flying Scotsman*, then numbered British Railways 60103, through Welwyn whilst in British Railways ownership was on 14 January 1963 when it worked the 1.15 pm from Kings Cross to Leeds as far as Doncaster. This locomotive was to be seen on many more occasions on special trains after it became the property of Mr Alan Pegler.

As described above, the elimination of steam haulage to and from Kings Cross took longer than anticipated. However in the period 1962 to 1969 a considerable number of special trains hauled by steam locomotives of the 'home' Region were run whilst appropriate servicing facilities were still available. A summary of those reported is shown in Table 10.1.

As a matter of interest, since 1967, when British Railways placed a complete embargo on steam haulage, *Flying Scotsman* was the only exception. This was due to a contract entered into with the new owner, Mr Alan Pegler, under which it could run until 1972. However, in September 1969 it was shipped to America to remain there until brought back to this country by W. H. McAlpine in February 1973. By this time British Railways had allowed steam haulage on a few specified routes, though these did not include the East Coast Main Line through Welwyn. The final entry in Table 10.1 records an historic event – the very last steam locomotive to pass through Welwyn.

In the earlier days of the main line diesel locomotive era several manufacturers' prototype locomotives were to be seen through Welwyn on express duties.

Table 10.1   *Summary of steam-hauled special trains through Welwyn North to and from Kings Cross 1962–9*

Date	Locomotive	Train	Date	Locomotive	Train
1962			**1964** (*continued*)		
28 March	A4 4-6-2 60007 *Sir Nigel Gresley*	Charter special to Retford	3 October	A3 4-6-2 4472 *Flying Scotsman*	Enthusiasts special to Darlington
11 April } 18 April } 26 April }	A4 4-6-2 60022 *Mallard*	Specials to Doncaster	4 October	Cl 7 4-6-2 70020 *Mercury*	Enthusiasts special to York
			24 October	A4 4-6-2 60009 *Union of South Africa*	'Jubilee Requiem' special to Newcastle
3 May	A4 4-6-2 60022 *Mallard*	Pullman charter to Harrogate			
19 May {	A3 4-6-2 60066 *Merry Hampton*	Enthusiasts special to Doncaster	**1966**		
{	A4 4-6-2 60017 *Silver Fox*	Return from Doncaster	20 October	Merchant Navy 35026 *Lamport and Holt Line*	Light engine to York
2 June	A4 4-6-2 60022 *Mallard*	'Aberdeen Flyer' as far as Edinburgh	22 October	A3 4-6-2 4472 *Flying Scotsman*	Enthusiasts special to York
2 July	A3 4-6-2 60103 *Flying Scotsman*	Royal Show special to Newcastle	**1967**		
			12 March	K4 2-6-0 3442 *The Great Marquess*	Light engine through Welwyn *en route* to SR
1963			30 April	A3 4-6-2 4472 *Flying Scotsman*	Charter to Chesterfield
24 February	A4 4-6-2 60022 *Mallard*	West Countryman rail tour	20 May } 21 May }	A3 4-6-2 4472 *Flying Scotsman*	Enthusiasts specials
27 March	V2 2-6-2 60862	Lincolnshire Handicap race special	2 June	A4 4-6-2 4498 *Sir Nigel Gresley*	Light engine through Welwyn *en route* to SR
29 March	B1 4-6-0 61097	From Grimsby with Chinese trade delegation	3 June	A3 4-6-2 4472 *Flying Scotsman*	Special from Newcastle
20 April	A3 4-6-2 60036 *Colombo*	Women's Organisations special from the W. Riding	17 June	A3 4-6-2 4472 *Flying Scotsman*	Special to Newcastle
8 June	Jubilee 4-6-0 45597 *Barbados*	Charter from Bradford	17 September	Castle 4-6-0 7029 *Clun Castle*	Special to Leeds
9 June	Coronation 4-6-2 46245 *City of London*	Special to Doncaster and return	8 October	Castle 4-6-0 7029 *Clun Castle*	Special to York
6 July	A4 4-6-2 60007 *Sir Nigel Gresley*	Mallard commemorative railtour to Doncaster and return	18 November	A3 4-6-2 4472 *Flying Scotsman*	Special to Chesterfield
30 September	A1 4-6-2 60140 *Balmoral*	Scarborough for Labour Party conference	**1968**		
5 October	B12/3 4-6-0 61572	Wandering 1500 rail tour to Stratford-on-Avon	1 May	A3 4-6-2 4472 *Flying Scotsman*	Non-stop special to Edinburgh on 40th anniversary of first non-stop 'Flying Scotsman' train
19 October	A3 4-6-2 4472 *Flying Scotsman*	Bassetlaw Conservative Association special to Kings Cross	6 October	A3 4-6-2 4472 *Flying Scotsman*	Yorkshire Harvester tour to York
1964			**1969**		
2 May	A3 4-6-2 60106 *Flying Fox*	Enthusiasts special to Doncaster	17 May	A3 4-6-2 4472 *Flying Scotsman*	To Diss
6 June	A3 4-6-2 60051 *Blink Bonny*	Enthusiasts special to Doncaster	18 August	A3 4-6-2 4472 *Flying Scotsman*	Light engine to Hornsey for SR tour to Liverpool
30 August	A3 4-6-2 4472 *Flying Scotsman*	Enthusiasts special to Doncaster	31 August	A3 4-6-2 4472 *Flying Scotsman*	Return special to Newcastle

In January 1959 the prototype English Electric 3300 hp Deltic arrived at Kings Cross for trials and for a short time was to be seen on the crack expresses through Welwyn. This locomotive was, of course, the forerunner of the famous 'Deltic' Class, numbering twenty-two, all of which were used on East Coast Main Line duties from 1961 until the last day of December 1981. For the record, 'Deltic' is on permanent display at the Science Museum, South Kensington.

The next prototype to arrive was an English Electric 2700 hp Co-Co No DP2 which from July 1963 was extensively used on the 10.10 am Kings Cross to Edinburgh returning on the 10.30 pm from Edinburgh. DP2 continued to work (except for a visit to works in 1965/6) other East Coast services until July 1967 when it returned to the makers.

Also in 1963 a Birmingham Carriage and Wagon Co 2750 bhp locomotive No D0260 named *Lion* and painted white, entered service but its appearances at Welwyn were less frequent than DP2 and it was not seen after February 1964. Both locomotives hauled the 'Yorkshire Pullman' at times. The Brush Traction Co (Hawker-Siddeley Group) produced a 4000 bhp Co-Co prototype locomotive No HS4000 named *Kestrel* in 1967 which was to be seen through Welwyn until March 1970 on Kings Cross to Newcastle expresses and the Hull to Stratford Freightliner train.

The introduction of diesel-electric locomotives in 1958, for both main line and outer suburban services is referred to in Chapters 6 and 11, and for the record it is sufficient to tabulate those classes of locomotives which were specifically allocated for the services to and from Kings Cross. (*See* Table 10.2.)

An unusual visitor to the East Coast Main Line was WR diesel-hydraulic locomotive D1023 *Western Fusilier* which worked a special from Kings Cross to York and back on 20 November 1976.

Table 10.2   *Types of diesel electric locomotives used on train services to and from Kings Cross*

Description	Power (hp)	Original numbers commencing	Class type
(a) Main line services			
English Electric Type 4	2000	D200	40
BR/Sulzer Type 4	2500	D138	46
Brush Type 4	2750	D1500	47
English Electric Type 5 'Deltic'	3300	D9000	55
(b) Suburban services			
BTH/Paxman Type 1	800	D8200	15
English Electric Type 1	1000	D8000	20
North British Locomotive Co Type 2	1000	D6100	21
English Electric Type 2 'Baby Deltic'	1100	D5900	23
BR/Sulzer Type 2	1160	D5000	24
BRCW Type 2	1160	D5300	26
Brush Type 2	1470	D5500	31
BRCW/Sulzer Type 3	1550	D6500	33

Figure 10.7   *BR Cl. 37 diesel-electric locomotive No D6748 hauling a Cleethorpes to Kings Cross express through Welwyn Garden City on 19 October 1963*
© *H. J. Stull*

An early foretaste of things to come on the Great Northern line through Welwyn occurred during mid-1977 when HST unit 253 026 from the Western Region worked the 0815 special from Gleneagles to Kings Cross on 13 June conveying heads of government returning from a weekend at the famous hotel. The same unit was used on 23 July on the 0740 from Kings Cross to Edinburgh and back, a charter excursion of The Prince's Trust/Lea Valley Railway Club 'Silver Jubilee Special'. This was the first HST to run from Kings Cross to Edinburgh.

From 1982 as a result of the large scale introduction of Inter-City 125 HSTs and electrification of both the inner and outer suburban services, diesel-locomotive haulage was confined to freight, parcels and permanent-way trains, a few Peterborough commuter services and overnight passenger trains, mostly hauled by either Class 31 or 47 locomotives. (*See* Figure 11.8.)

For the electric services between Moorgate/Kings Cross and Hertford North, Letchworth and Welwyn Garden City sixty-four 75 mph Class 313 3-car units were supplied in 1976 but after 1982 only forty-eight units were required to work the peak services. These units were unique in that they were fitted for dual voltage working, with retractable pantographs for picking up a.c. current from overhead wires and with fixed collector shoes for use on the d.c. third rail section between Drayton Park and Moorgate. More recently they have been fitted with radio apparatus for contacting the Central Control in connection with driver-only operation. (*See* Figure 3.9.)

For the Kings Cross to Royston services, twenty-six Class 312 4-car units (*See* Plate 4) with a maximum speed of 90 mph were used but these were to be replaced in stages from Spring 1986 by twenty-four faster-accelerating 100 mph Class 317/2 units, similar to those used on the Moorgate to Bedford service, to enable full one-man-operated trains to be used for Great Northern electric services, except that the Class 313 trains between Finsbury Park and Moorgate continued to be operated with guards. British Rail (letter to the authors of 23 December 1985) asserts that this is a Department of Transport requirement.

The Department of Transport (letter to the authors of 21 January 1986) say that this was British Rail's own proposal.

The new Class 317 units, known as 317/2 on the Great Northern line, are of 4-coach formations with fully automatic 'tightlock' couplers enabling a maximum of twelve coaches to be run as one train, although eight coaches is the maximum intended. Each 4-coach unit has seating for 273 second class and twenty-two first class passengers, and a single high-powered motor car with four traction motors electronically controlled. Air (disc) brakes, self-levelling air suspension, power-operated sliding doors (with passenger press buttons) and public address equipment are incorporated in the design. The coach bodies are based on the Mark 3 HST coaches where any opening in the body weakens it, hence the small number of doors as compared with the Class 312 units of traditional underframe construction.

Differences between these and the Bedford Class 317 units include a top speed increased from 90 mph to 100 mph to

Figure 10.8   *Class 317/2 electric multiple units (EMUs) Nos 354 and 349 passing Welwyn North station on a special train carrying civic dignitaries from Kings Cross to Royston on 3 March 1986*   © *T. W. Gladwin*

improve the traffic flow through the Welwyn bottleneck (the speed limit through the tunnels being only 105 mph), first class accommodation, and a lockable parcels area with tip-up seats immediately next to the driver's cab. A demonstration run, principally for civic officials, took 39 minutes non-stop from Kings Cross to Royston on 3 March 1986. On the return journey the train stopped at Brookmans Park for guests to attend the 'first sod' cutting ceremony at the site of the new Welham Green station.

Electrification of the Great Northern line beyond Hitchin to Leeds, Newcastle and Edinburgh is now (1986) being carried out. Electric services to Peterborough are planned to commence in May 1987, using the Class 317/2 multiple-unit driver-only operated trains. Electrification to Leeds is scheduled for October 1989 and to Newcastle and Edinburgh in May 1991. These services are likely to be hauled by Class 91 Electra 140 mph locomotives of which thirty-one have been ordered by British Rail at over £1 million each. For these electrical equipment will be supplied by GEC and mechanised parts will be supplied and final assembly done by a British Rail Engineering Works, probably Crewe. Freight services may be hauled by Class 87/2 locomotives more of which are to be constructed for the West Coast Main Line.

As a prelude to these services, on Sunday 14 September 1986 Class 87/1 electric locomotive 87101 *Stephenson* worked a test train consisting of eight sleeping cars and two Mark III coaches from Kings Cross to Letchworth, returning via Hertford North to London. This was the first electric locomotive-hauled train on the East Coast Main Line.

From this chapter it will be appreciated that the ECML through Welwyn has always provided a unique opportunity to observe a wide variety of motive power; even so the foregoing catalogue does not claim to be complete and doubtless the observant reader will be able to recall more instances of unusual locomotives within the classes quoted and additional classes not

Table 10.3 *The number of all train movements through Welwyn North according to type of motive power, 1980–6*

Type of train	Number of all train movements including passenger, freight, parcels, empty coaching stock, and light locomotives		
	17 June 1980	16 June 1984	17 July 1986
(a) Locomotive hauled			
Class 31	19	8	14
Class 37	2	—	1
Class 40	1	—	—
Class 46	11	—	—
Class 47	34	58	48
Class 55	24	—	—
Total:	**91**	**66**	**63**
(b) InterCity 125 High Speed Trains	64	91	92
(c) Electric Multiple Units (EMUs)			
Class 312	134	121	44
Class 313	4	8	19
Class 317	—	—	65*
Total:	**138**	**129**	**128**
(d) Diesel Multiple Units (DMUs)	—	—	1
Total train movements:	**293**	**286**	**284**

*Three Class 317 movements were cancelled on 17 July 1986 due to a temporary power failure.

referred to which have passed over Digswell Viaduct between 1850 and the present time.

In recent years there has been a considerable reduction in the variety of motive power and train types passing Welwyn North as British Railways standardised on fewer classes. This reduction is evident from Table 10.3 which shows the number of train movements according to the type of motive power which passed through Welwyn North during the 24 hours of the days shown.

Chapter 11

Coaching Stock

History shows that the Great Northern Railway was the first to develop certain types of coaching stock. For example, in 1879 it ran a restaurant car and in 1882 it built the first side-corridor coach, that is, a coach with a corridor which did not connect through a vestibule to the next coach. However, such vehicles did not carry passengers to and from Welwyn, at least not until they had run on other services for very many years. The typical coaches on the London to Hitchin, Cambridge and Peterborough trains prior to 1914 would have been oil- or gas-lit 4- and 6-wheelers. They had rudimentary springing and were devoid of heat and lavatories. (*See* Figure 11.1.) The GNR Works at Doncaster built such coaches in great numbers and they lasted for many years even after they were drafted away from London. As late as the early 1870s the GNR was still building 6-wheeled stock for the East Coast Main Line service. These coaches, which ran in the varnished teak livery of the East Coast Joint Stock, were used on all the best through trains to and from Scotland. Such stock was paid for jointly by the GNR, North Eastern and North British Railways. It is significant that when the London & North Eastern Railway brought the Stirling single-driver No 1 back into service in 1938 to head a train of Victorian rolling stock built in 1888, which it displayed alongside the new stock built for the 'Flying Scotsman', the authorities had no difficulty in finding the coaches to run behind No 1. They merely had to refurbish the regular stock then in use on a couple of Lincolnshire branch lines. One writer described the 1888 stock used in 1938 as 'replicas'. This was not the case as some rural travellers would willingly have testified.

The architect of these vehicles was E. F. Howlden who was appointed Carriage and Wagon Superintendent in 1877. He was followed by H. N. Gresley in 1905, who soon made his mark as his first design with the characteristic elliptical roof and electric lighting appeared in that year. The famous Gresley bogie followed in 1908. Gresley is also remembered for his liking for articulation (that is, one bogie to support the ends of two vehicles) and many carriages incorporating all these features were to be used by Welwyn passengers, if not immediately they were introduced, then within a few years.

Nigel Gresley clearly had excellent ideas on designing rolling stock to give passengers a comfortable and safe ride through the use both of his bogie design and of the Gould buckeye coupler, a life saving device which prevented countless casu-

Figure 11.1 *A typical GNR outer suburban train passing Greenwood signal box' near Hadley Wood station, hauled by Class D2 4–4–0 No 1312. Note the first three coaches are six-wheelers* Courtesy Real Photographs Co

alties by keeping GNR and LNER coaches upright and unaffected by telescoping when any derailment occurred. As far as Welwyn passengers were concerned, there were never enough Gresley coaches built and while some early Gresley non-corridor bogie coaches to GNR designs were eventually included in trains calling at Welwyn, along with the long lived 6-wheelers, it was not until well into the LNER era that Gresley-designed coaches made up a complete train.

Two of the Gresley articulated twins built in 1923, which included lavatories with access via side corridors, are shown in Figure 11.2 calling at Welwyn Garden City in 1938. Articulated twins of the later standard LNER design were introduced in the 1930s. These formed the mainstay of the outer suburban

Figure 11.3 *The 1.56 pm Kings Cross to Cambridge train including a Gresley LNER luggage van, two BR Mark 1 coaches and a Thompson LNER luggage van in its formation, hauled by LNER 'Sandringham' Class 4–6–0 No 61652* Darlington. *Shown approaching Stapleford on 31 August 1958, having been diverted to the Hertford loop line*   © J. F. Aylard

Figure 11.2 *Early Gresley articulated-twin, non-corridor coaches forming a Cambridge to Kings Cross train, entering Welwyn Garden City station behind Class C1 'Atlantic' No 4439 on 19 June 1938. Note that an empty restaurant car is at the rear of the train*   © T. Middlemass

services from Kings Cross and many other similar services throughout the LNER system until the mid-1950s.

Gresley also designed a range of non-articulated non-corridor coaches which were widely used by the LNER, and some came to the Kings Cross area for outer suburban work. However, one that is particularly remembered by travellers in steam-hauled days is the composite two-class semi-corridor design, which appeared in 1947 after Gresley's death and in the last days of the LNER. They were of all-steel construction and, while they had Gresley bogies, clearly carried the imprint of Edward Thompson, his successor as Chief Mechanical Engineer at Doncaster. They were flush-sided with square-cornered corridor and compartment windows and – the most obvious sign of a Thompson coach – a white oval toilet window. Some of these plus some similar all third class coaches came new to the outer suburban services straight from the private builders, Cravens and Pickering respectively. At that time the railway's own works at Doncaster and York were fully occupied building corridor coaches. Any new vehicles in the austere post-war days made a more than usual impact and the fact that they had 6' 4" wide compartments made them doubly welcome. Welwyn North passengers were lucky to be so honoured by the company which had long forced them to ride in second-string vehicles. These were the envy of inner suburban passengers who had to continue to make do with their so called 'bogie locals' for many years longer.

Another variety of Gresley stock familiar to Welwyn passengers was the 8-coach 'bogie local' sets (as they were known in GNR and LNER days – in British Railways' time the name was 'quad arts'). These were made up of two sets of four non-corridor coaches articulated on five bogies. (*See* Figures 10.4 and 11.4.) These were designed solely as 'people movers', rather than for comfort, although they rode superbly at any speed and were designed to fit into the platforms at Moorgate. On the main line they were used principally on local services to Hatfield and later to Welwyn Garden City. However, they were occasionally seen at Welwyn North on the slower off-peak trains and in times when there was any disruption to the normal coach rosters. During the thick fogs and smogs that featured before the Clean Air Act, these sets conveyed as many as nine hundred people, eighteen to a compartment – far more than any other type of GNR coach could cope with at a single lift.

In 1954 BR built a range of all-steel non-corridor coaches and four types were used on the Eastern Region. Two of these, the composite and open second, included lavatories. All four types came new to Kings Cross where they were formed into sets for the outer suburban services (*see* Figure 10.5) on which they lasted until the full electrification of the line in 1978. In some ways, despite being new and of all-steel construction, they represented a step backwards in carriage design as far as the GN main line was concerned. The buckeye coupler was aban-

Figure 11.4   *BR Cl. 21 diesel-electric locomotive No D6100, built by the North British Locomotive Company, on an up inner suburban train composed of two Gresley 'bogie local' (Quad-art) sets approaching New Barnet station on 15 May 1959*
© *J. F. Aylard*

Figure 11.5   *BR Cl. 26 diesel-electric locomotive No D5330, supplied by Sulzer, on the 7.35 am train from Baldock to Kings Cross on 11 August 1959. It is seen approaching New Barnet hauling a six-coach corridor train with two BR outer suburban non-corridor coaches in front*   © *J. F. Aylard*

doned in favour of screw couplings because the speeds at which the coaches were expected to run did not justify these expensive fittings. This disregarded the fact that they would have to share the track with, at that time, high-speed trains and there was no way that the authorities could guarantee that the BR coaches would not be in collision with one of the faster trains. As will be mentioned later, Welwyn North passengers were lucky not to be involved in just such a collision with BR screw-coupling stock.

These coaches using BR B1 bogies based on the GWR design for reasons of accessibility, had a comparatively poor reputation for rough riding and noise. The best that could be said of the new vehicles was that they had compartments either 6' 1" or 6' 3" wide as against 5' 3½" in the 'quad art' sets and 6' 2" in the articulated twins. None the less only the first class compartments had armrests and shoulder lights.

Some sets serving Welwyn North after 1945 were regularly formed of LNER standard main line corridor coaches (*see* Figure 11.3). Although these gave an excellent ride, by the time they had been relegated to appear regularly on stopping trains at Welwyn North, they were long outdated both in style and the low wattage of the lighting. One such train was sadly involved

Figure 11.7 *Three BR Cl. 105 twin diesel multiple unit (DMUs) sets on an up Cambridge to Kings Cross train diverted through Gordon Hill in May 1959. These units were extensively used on the inner and outer suburban services* © *J. F. Aylard*

in the accident at Welwyn Garden City on 7 January 1957 when the 6.18 am Baldock to Kings Cross was run into by the 7.10 pm Aberdeen to Kings Cross sleeper just south of the station. Once again the buckeye coupler prevented telescoping and there was only one death. Between 1935 and 1957 there were three major accidents between Digswell and Welwyn Garden City. In each case the Ministry of Transport reported that lives had been saved by the buckeye coupler.

In February 1959 diesel locomotives of various types were introduced on the outer suburban services. Those supplied by Brush (Class 31) and Sulzer (Class 26) proved excellent. Unfortunately, like the Type 2 'Baby Deltics' (Class 23) supplied by

Figure 11.6 *BR Cl. 23 'Baby Deltic' diesel-electric locomotive No D5909 on a down stopping train at Welwyn North station on 18 July 1959* © *D. E. White*

English Electric, the new Type 2 locomotives (Class 21) built by the North British Locomotive Company proved very unreliable. (*See* Figures 11.4 and 11.6.) The steam-hauled rolling stock hauled by these new locomotives was not, however, changed. Craven-built Diesel Multiple Units (DMUs) (*see* Figures 11.7 and 11.9) with open saloon type bodies appeared on the inner suburban services in 1958 and these subsequently began to filter on to the Welwyn North off-peak services. In June 1968 and in May 1969 other high density DMUs with compartment-type coaches, Rolls Royce engines and BR's last hydraulic transmission, were transferred to Kings Cross for use on the inner and outer suburban services. Thus from May 1969 to October 1977 Welwyn North was served by the three types of DMU plus the locomotive-hauled standard BR corridor and non-corridor coaches.

On 8 November 1976, the inner suburban service was electrified using Class 313 units. Services from the GN lines to Broad Street and to Moorgate via Farringdon were withdrawn on the previous Saturday together with the least reliable high-density DMUs. On 3 October 1977 a few sets of newly delivered Class 312 Electric Multiple Units (EMUs), designed for the outer suburban service, were introduced on duties based on the former diesel-train timings. As a consequence of the introduction of large numbers of Class 313 and fewer 312 units, much of the older rolling stock was withdrawn and the remainder reallocated to other duties. Stock withdrawn included the BR locomotive-hauled non-corridor coaches which were the last to remain in use anywhere on BR. The last workings of this stock, on 30 September 1977, were the 1742 and 1746 departures from Kings Cross to Royston (arr. 1848) and Hitchin (arr. 1836) respectively. The latter called at Welwyn North at 1816. Reallocated units included the Craven and one of the high-density DMUs which were no longer required on the inner suburban services. These, the more reliable units, were formed into longer formations than hitherto and used on the outer suburban services to fill the gaps not covered by the few EMUs then

available. From 3 October 1977 to 5 February 1978, Welwyn North passengers not fortunate enough to catch one of the new electrics would have usually travelled in the aged, noisy and vibrant diesel units, or occasionally in the dated BR standard Mark 1 corridor coaches on a through Kings Cross to Cambridge train.

From 6 February 1978 the Class 312 EMUs took over all services to and from Welwyn North. For the first time since 1850 Welwyn North passengers benefitted from a one hundred per cent new and uniform fleet of vehicles of modern design. This class ruled supreme for eight years, being among the most reliable 25 kv EMU in BR service. Initially, calculated on a failure rate per 100 000 miles, the Class 312/1 units based at Clacton proved ten times more reliable than the Class 312/0 units on the GN outer suburban services. This is officially attributed to 'differences in route and stopping patterns' and 'to weaknesses

Figure 11.8   *BR Cl. 31 diesel-electric locomotives built by Brush Traction, north of New Barnet on 11 March 1961. On the right is No D5601 on an up BR five-coach non-corridor inner suburban train being overtaken by No D5608 on a Cambridge to Broad Street (Saturdays only) train*   © *J. F. Aylard*

in the Hornsey maintenance performance'. In contrast the newer Class 313 units, used principally on inner suburban trains between Moorgate and Welwyn Garden City, were reported in 1980 to have the highest failure rate on the Eastern Region (*Monopolies Commission Report on British Railways Board London and South East Commuter Services*. HMSO 1980 Cmnd 8046). From 1 October 1985 one northbound service a day, stopping at Welwyn North, has been operated by one of these units.

From May 1986 new Class 317/2 EMUs started to take over the services operated between Kings Cross, Letchworth and Royston by the Class 312s, thereby releasing some, but not all of the latter for transfer to lines out of Liverpool Street.

Welwyn North being a main line station, whenever electric services are disrupted HST and other diesel-powered trains may be required to stop there, adding further to the variety of coaches used by passengers in the district.

Figure 11.9   *BR Craven-built diesel multiple unit train between the Welwyn tunnels on 12 April 1971*   © *G. W. Goslin*

Chapter 12

Accidents

The section of the railway through Welwyn has fortunately been relatively free of major accidents. There have however been several important exceptions.

Accounts of several early accidents in the Welwyn area are given by Wrottesley (1979). The first occurred on 4 May 1864 when the points were switched under the 1.30 pm from Kings Cross as it was still entering the Hertford branch. The third and last coach were derailed.

Another more serious accident, seven months later, is described by Wrottesley (1979) as follows:

> On 7 December 1864 the 2.20 pm 'pick-up' from Peterborough was to be shunted at Welwyn for an up Manchester express to pass. There was some confusion between the head and rear guards. In the darkness the latter turned the points for the down siding instead of the up. In consequence the train backed across the down line. The down main signals were flung to danger, but too late to prevent the 7 pm Midland train from colliding with the wagons. Fourteen passengers were injured, some severely. Both lines were blocked for 2½ hours until single line working was possible.

At about 11.20 pm on 9 June 1866 the locomotive hauling a northbound train of thirty-eight empty coal wagons and guard's van failed and came to a halt in Welwyn North Tunnel when a boiler tube burst allowing water on to the fire with a resultant loss of power. At about 11.36 pm a following Midland goods train of twenty-six goods wagons and guard's van bound for Bedford via Hitchin approached Welwyn; the line from Bedford to St Pancras had not then been constructed. The train slowed against signals set at danger but continued when both the distant and station signals were cleared and entered the south tunnel at about twenty to twenty-five miles per hour. Minutes later it ran into the rear of the stationary train. The Midland locomotive was derailed and debris piled up on both tracks. The driver and fireman were still attempting to get clear of this train when a Great Northern fast up goods of thirty-one wagons and two vans ran into the wreckage. About four hours later a fire started which was to burn until the afternoon of the 11th. This appeared to have been caused by burning naphtha from workmen's lamps dropping into a truck load of furniture packed in shavings. The tunnel was not cleared until 9.30 pm on the 11th and traffic through it recommenced at 3 am on the 12th, forty-one hours after the accident. Joseph Wray, the guard of the train that failed, was killed by the first collision and John Rawlins, a former GNR employee who was illegally riding in the van with Wray, died of his injuries. Lacey, the guard of the up train, received serious injuries. Although the fact was not referred to in the official report, the up train was conveying meat which should have been transferred to another service at Peterborough. Its fateful journey was therefore by chance! (*See* Figure 12.1.)

The following extracts from the report of the accident which appeared in *The Times* of 12 June 1866 are particularly interesting.

> Simple and obvious as are the causes of this unprecedented catastrophe it would seem that it could not by any possibility have occurred had there not been at least two or three breaches of the regulations issued by the company for the guidance of their servants and the safety of the public. These regulations on the Great Northern are generally regarded as singularly clear and good, and hence in some degree is to be attributed the comparative immunity from serious accidents which this line has hitherto enjoyed. The infraction of the rules referred to, and the consequences to which it led, will become more apparent as we describe in a manner to be intelligible the precise nature of the accident, which, as has been observed, is without parallel in the annals of railway disasters.

The report in *The Times* then cites the possible breaches of the regulations whilst attributing most of the blame for the accident to Joseph Wray as follows:

> Now, it was evidently the first duty of the guard on this accident occurring, to hasten back with his lamp and prevent the approach of any other train on the same line of rails. As the body of this unfortunate man – Joseph Wray – was found close to his brake, at the rear of the train, it is pretty clear that this regulation, which is common to all railways alike, was neglected by him, and dearly did he pay for his neglect, for he now lies a mangled corpse at the Railway Arms Inn, near the station.

As correctly stated in the *Illustrated London News* of 16 June 1866 the 'Railway Arms Inn' referred to in *The Times* was in fact the Cowper Arms where the inquest was held.

As evidenced by the official report, *The Times*' analysis of the

Figure 12.1   *The scene in Welwyn North (Harmer Green) Tunnel following the accident on 9 June 1866, from a lithograph in the Illustrated London News dated 16 June 1866*

Courtesy of the Illustrated London News

accident was substantially correct. The inquiry into the accident was made by Captain F. H. Rich RE who reported on the signalling procedures that had occurred as follows:

> When the Midland down goods approached Welwyn about 11.36 pm, the signalman at that station had not received the telegraphic notification from Knebworth that the train of empties which he had allowed into the tunnel at 11.20 pm had passed Knebworth, and therefore, before lowering his signals for the Midland goods, he telegraphed to the Knebworth signalman, to know if the train that entered at 11.20 had passed out. The Knebworth signalman stated most positively that he answered "No;" but the Welwyn signalman stated with equal decision that he received "Yes" in reply, and consequently that he lowered the signals for the Midland goods to pass in. This answer was received at 11.36 pm, but the Welwyn signalman, considering that the telegraph announcing that the train of empties had passed Knebworth must have been sent at 11.30 pm, when he was attending to the telegraphs relating to an up train, and that he must have missed observing it, entered the reply to his question as if he had received the telegraph notifying that the empties had passed Knebworth at 11.30 pm. This was an incorrect entry, which he should not have made, and I am inclined to believe that the answer that he received was "No," but that in the hurry of the moment he read the "No" as "Out," which are [*sic*] somewhat similar on the telegraph instrument. "Out" would bear the same significance to him at that time as "Yes." The Welwyn signalman also disobeyed his instructions by the manner in which he asked whether the 11.20 train had passed out of the tunnel. He should have merely telegraphed to Knebworth, "train waiting."
>
> The telegraph working at Welwyn and Knebworth is done with a single instrument, which is a speaking instrument with "Out" and "In" marked on it. The needle is pushed to the same side for "Out" and for "No;" the number of beats being the difference between them, and I think the Welwyn signalman mistook the reply sent from Knebworth.
>
> The Knebworth signalman is borne out in his statement that he answered "No" by his refusing to acknowledge the "train in" signal which was given by the Welwyn signalman at 11.38 pm for the Midland goods. It is possible that he may have hastily replied "Yes," and immediately afterwards recollected, that there was a train in the tunnel, which was the case a short time since at Whitehaven; but I am more inclined to believe that the mistake was made by the signalman at Welwyn. I do believe that both

signalmen intended to speak the truth, and that each feels confident in his own mind that the other committed the mistake.

The signalmen involved were James Bradford at Welwyn and Joseph Harding at Knebworth. At the inquest into the deaths of Joseph Wray and John Rawlins the jury did not take it upon themselves to attribute blame to either signalmen. Captain Rich in his report finally summarised the cause of the accident and the mistakes that occurred, and made recommendations as follows:

This melancholy accident was caused by the neglect of guard Wray, who appears to have remained quietly in his van at the tail of the train of empties for about 16 minutes after his train came to a stand, instead of obeying the regulations of the Great Northern Railway Company, which specially provide that the guards in such cases shall proceed back one mile to protect their trains, or till they meet another servant of the company, with whom they can arrange for the safety of their train, and that they shall not trust to the protection of the telegraph. Secondly, a mistake occurs between the signalmen stationed at the north and south ends of the tunnels, who are charged with the protection of the interval by the telegraph, and who are not permitted to allow two trains travelling in the same direction to be in the interval between their stations at the same time.

The Great Northern Railway Company are changing their system of telegraph. It is very desirable for them to do so and to adopt instruments for working the line which shall have the means of blocking over the needle to 'line clear' or 'line blocked', and to have separate speaking instruments.

I would also recommend a strict enforcing of the regulation that requires guards to go back at once to protect their trains where they are stopped by unavoidable accident, as on the 9th inst.

There is no doubt that this most necessary precaution for the safe working of all railways is too often neglected.

While the line through Welwyn was blocked stopping trains from Kings Cross were routed via Hertford (Cowbridge), Cambridge, Royston and Hitchin, and express trains via Hertford, Cambridge, March and Peterborough.

Another accident in the following year is described by Wrottesley (1979) as follows:

An up goods train arrived at Welwyn junction just before 5 pm on 5 November 1867 and began to shunt. Part was detached, and set back on the Hertford branch and through some points into an up siding. The engine and some wagons then returned to the main line ready to set back on the remainder. The guard accidentally set the points for the down main line and called his train back. A down passenger train was approaching, which hit the wagons at 40 mph. Some passengers received injuries and several vehicles were damaged. The signalman had endeavoured, too late, to divert the passenger train on to the Luton branch. This accident again clearly demonstrated the urgent necessity for interlocking points and signals and concentrating operation of points on running lines under signalmen's control.

On Friday 6 February 1920 a collision occurred in Welwyn North Tunnel. Trains were diverted via the new Hertford loop, the first time main line passenger trains had travelled over this section.

The next major collision which also involved three trains occurred on 9 December 1930. This accident, in dense fog, happened about noon and just south of Twentieth Mile Bridge, Welwyn Garden City. An up coal train from Peterborough to Ferme Park (Hornsey), hauled by Class O1 2-8-0 No 3468, ran into the rear of a stationary ballast train on the up slow line. The coal train's locomotive fell on to the adjacent Hertford to Hatfield single line, at the same time scattering a mass of debris on the up goods and up main lines. A few minutes later an up fast goods train bound for London, and hauled by Class K3 2-6-0 No 4001, collided with the wreckage with the result that wagons were piled three high and spread to block the down lines also. Only the Hatfield-to-Luton single line was unaffected, and this was used for a shuttle service of trains between Hatfield and Welwyn Garden City. The main lines were reopened on Friday 11 December. The only casualty was a guard who suffered minor facial injuries.

An unusual accident occurred at Digswell Junction, immediately south of Welwyn Viaduct, on 29 September 1931. At 6.40 pm a returning race special from Newmarket to Kings Cross, hauled by Class C1 4-4-2 No 4436, became derailed as it passed over the points leading to the up goods line. As a consequence of the closure of Digswell signal box alterations to the signalling were being made at the time but the electrical work had not been completed. An inspector instructed the signalman at Welwyn North, Mr Bygrave, to pull the lever actuating the points, which ought to have been clipped (locked), but did not appreciate that the train had not completely cleared them.

The official report on the accident attributes no blame to the signalman. Although the first three coaches had successfully crossed the points, the fourth was derailed and the rest took the goods line without derailment. Fortunately the train had been checked (slowed) by earlier signals and was travelling at only about 25 mph. All the coaches remained upright, principally because of the action of the driver in bringing the train to a standstill by a careful application of the brake, and because

Figure 12.3   LNER Class K3 2–6–0 No 4009 immediately following the accident at Welwyn Garden City on 15 June 1935   © *Welwyn Times*

Figure 12.2   Smashed coaches following the accident at Welwyn Garden City on 15 June 1935   © *Welwyn Times*

the coaches were fitted with buckeye couplers. There were no casualties.

Another accident of importance occurred at Welwyn Garden City on 15 June 1935 as a result of a lapse on the part of a signalman who allowed more than one train into a section. Fourteen people lost their lives in this incident when the locomotive, LNER Class K3 2-6-0 No 4009, hauling the 10.58 pm Kings Cross to Leeds mail train ran into the rear of the 10.53 pm Kings Cross to Newcastle hauled by Class C1 4-4-2 No 4441. As a result of this accident a modification to track circuiting was made here and at other sites with similar installations. Under the modified system, which became known as 'the Welwyn Control' (*see* Chapter 5), once a train has been offered to the next signal box that box cannot give 'line clear' to the offering box until the track circuit has been occupied and cleared. The 'line clear' can then be given and the next train accepted. Only then can the offering box signalman operate his starting signal, thus allowing the train to enter the next section.

The last major accident occurred on 7 January 1957 when the 7.10 pm overnight sleeper from Aberdeen, hauled by Class A2 4-6-2 No 60520 *Owen Tudor*, passed three sets of adverse signals and ran into the rear of the 6.18 am outer suburban train from Baldock hauled by LNER Class L1 2-6-4T No 67741. The latter had just left Welwyn Garden City at 7.12 am and had crossed to the up fast line for its non-stop run to Finsbury Park. In the official report of the accident it was estimated that the speed of the express train at the time of impact was 60 to 65 mph and that of the outer suburban train 30 to 35 mph. There was no reason to believe that any of the signals were not operating properly but as a result of the accident colour light signals replaced the semaphore arms at the south end of Digswell Viaduct. Unfortunately one Welwyn Garden City passenger travelling in the last coach of the suburban train was killed.

Several minor accidents, two of which occurred at Ayot, have also been recorded.

On 19 January 1875 an up goods train left Luton for Hatfield just in advance of the 7.35 pm passenger train and stalled on the incline short of Ayot. The driver placed detonators at the rear of his train to protect it and again attempted to ascend the bank. By then, however, the following passenger train had arrived, smashing into the disabled goods train, and derailing the passenger train locomotive which rolled down the embankment before its boiler exploded. There were no deaths. (Woodward 1977).

Ayot was the scene of a second accident during the General Strike of May 1926. On 8 May the afternoon goods train with fifteen wagons left Hatfield for Luton about 3.9 pm behind Class C12 4-4-2T No 1550. Unfortunately, as the station staff at Ayot had not been advised of the train's departure from Hatfield, the points were not set for the main single line but instead for the loop which was on a gradient and protected by a pair of catchpoints. Despite efforts by the driver, the locomotive and two of the wagons went through the catchpoints. The locomotive was overturned and came to rest at an angle of

Figure 12.4   *The scene at Ayot station following the derailment of LNER Class C12 4-4-2T No 1550 on 8 May 1926*   *Courtesy of Welwyn Garden City Library*

45° only a few yards from a steep bank. The volunteer crew received only minor injuries.

The story of the station at Ayot was prematurely concluded on 26 July 1948 when it was completely gutted by fire, leaving only the platforms. The station was not rebuilt but was closed to passenger traffic on 26 September 1949, well in advance of the branch closure to passengers on 26 April 1965 and completely in October 1970 when the Blackbridge tip near Wheathampstead closed. The latter had been used for dumping domestic waste from the Greater London Council depot at Ashburton Grove near Finsbury Park.

Whilst not strictly classed as accidents several incidents are recorded of trains being machine-gunned by enemy action from the air at Knebworth and on Welwyn Viaduct during the Second World War.

Chapter 13

Fares and Tickets

13.1 Fares

During the 72-year period of operation by the Great Northern Railway (1850–1922) fares remained almost constant.

In 1850, the first year of operation, passengers from Welwyn could travel to Kings Cross first, second or third class. Periodical tickets, now known as season tickets, were apparently not available to third class passengers. The prices of periodical tickets at the beginning of 1851 are set out in Table 13.1.

TABLE 13.1 *Prices of periodical tickets between Kings Cross and Welwyn in 1851*

Period (months)	Class	
	First	Second
	£ s. d	£ s. d
12	22 0 0	15 0 0
11	20 13 6	14 2 0
10	19 5 0	13 2 6
9	18 3 0	12 7 6
8	16 17 6	11 10 0
7	15 8 0	10 10 0
6	13 15 0	9 7 6

The ordinary passenger single fares from Welwyn to Kings Cross in 1850 were 3s 9d (1st), 2s 9d (2nd) and 1s 9d (3rd) but, as shown in Table 13.2, these were soon adjusted to 4s 0d, 3s 0d, and 1s 9½d respectively.

It is interesting to note (*see* Table 13.2) that passengers from Hitchin to Kings Cross were charged not only according to their chosen class of travel but also according to the type of train in which they travelled. Third class travel was available on the slow 'Ordinary' trains only.

TABLE 13.2 *Ordinary passenger single fares from Hitchin to Kings Cross in 1858*

Type of train	Class		
	First	Second	Third
	s d	s d	s d
Express	8 6	6 0	—
Mixed Express	6 6	5 0	—
Ordinary	6 0	4 6	2 8

A special 'Market Fare' of 1s 0d was available on specified trains for passengers travelling from Welwyn to Hitchin on market days. This was increased to 1s 1d in 1909.

In 1858 other charges from Welwyn to Kings Cross were as follows:

	s	d	
Carriage	8	3	
Horse	5	6	one or each
Dog	1	0	
Extra Luggage		0¼	per item

These charges remained unchanged until at least 1915.

The timetables and leaflets advertising such charges also described other facilities available at stations. Typically, the Great Northern Railway Timetable for 1907 referring to Welwyn states 'Flys are in attendance on the arrival of all trains from 11.10 am to 7.38 pm'.

Travellers between Welwyn and Kings Cross continued to have a choice of all three classes of travel until early in 1891 when second class facilities were removed from trains travelling north of New Barnet, but they were reinstated to Potters Bar from October 1915 and to Hatfield and Welwyn Garden City,

Plate 7 *LNER Class A3 'Pacific' No 60050* **Persimmon**, *as running from October 1961 until withdrawn from service in June 1962, with trough-type smoke deflectors, working the 8.45 am outer suburban train to Kings Cross* © *R. Malcolm James*

TABLE 13.3   *Examples of ordinary single and return fares between Welwyn North (formerly Welwyn) and Kings Cross*

Year	Single Fares			Return Fares		
	First	Second	Third	First	Second	Third
	s d	s d	s d	s d	s d	s d
1850	3 9	2 9	1 9			
1851	4 0	3 0	1 9½			
1860	4 0	3 0	1 10			
1870	4 0	3 0	1 10			
1875	3 6	2 7	1 10	6 9	5 0	3 8
1879	3 6	2 7	1 9½	6 9	5 0	3 7
1891	3 6	—	1 9½	6 9	—	3 7
1896	3 3	—	1 9½	6 6	—	3 7
1903	3 3	—	1 9½	6 3	—	3 7
1908	3 3	—	1 10	6 3	—	3 8
1915	3 3	—	1 10	6 3	—	3 8
1935	4 6½	—	2 9½	6 0	—	4 0
1940	4 6½	—	2 9½	9 1	—	5 6½
1950		—	3 11		—	7 10
1955	5 3	—		10 6	—	
1960	6 4	4 2	—	12 8	8 4	—
1965	8 3	5 6	—	16 6	11 0	—

					Second	
					Peak	Off Peak
1970	9 9	6 5	—	19 6	12 10	10 0
	£ p	£ p		£ p	£ p	£ p
1975	0 92	0 61		1 84	1 22	0 84
1978	1 95	1 30		3 90	2 60	1 62
1980	3 35	2 22		6 70	4 44	2 64
1984	4 10	2 70		8 20	5 40	3 20
1985	4 50	3 00		9 00	6 00	3 40
1986	4 80	3 20		9 60	6 40	3 60

NOTES: Second class facilities to Welwyn were withdrawn in 1891
Third class was reclassified second class in 1956
Most fares shown are for January in each year
Off Peak tickets are not available before 0930

when Inner Suburban trains were extended to these stations. Second class facilities on services to Hatfield and Welwyn

Garden City, and to Potters Bar were finally withdrawn in 1938 and March 1942 respectively, and third class was reclassified second class from 3 June 1956.

Periodical tickets became available for third class passengers in 1888. The first class return rates between Welwyn and Kings Cross set in 1874 of £24 3s 0d (12 months), £12 1s 6d (6 months) and £6 0s 9d (3 months) remained unchanged until after 1915. The equivalent second class rates up to 1891 were £16 16s 0d, £8 8s 0d and £4 4s 0d respectively. From 1891 until after 1915 the new third class rates were £13 16s 0d, £6 18s 0d and £3 9s 0d.

From March 1942, as part of wartime economy, most trains provided third class accommodation only. After the war first class provision was gradually increased although some third/second class only trains remained until the mid-1970s.

TABLE 13.4   *Comparison of season (periodical) ticket and ordinary fare prices between Welwyn North and Kings Cross from 1851 to 1986*

Ticket type	Fare			1986 fare as a percentage of 1915 fare
	1851	1915	1986	
Periodical/season tickets	£ s d	£ s d	£ p	
First class				
12 months	22 0 0	24 3 0	1428 00	5913
6 months	13 15 0	12 1 6	822 80	6814
3 months	—	6 0 9	411 40	6814
Second class*				
12 months	—	13 16 0	980 00	7101
6 months	—	6 18 0	564 60	8182
3 months	—	3 9 0	282 30	8182
Ordinary fares				
First class				
Single	4 0	3 3	4 80	2953
Return	?	6 3	9 60	3072
Second class*				
Single	1 10	1 10	3 20	3491
Return	?	3 8	6 40	3491

*Third class in 1851 and 1915

Table 13.4 provides a good measure of the fare values and increases up to 1986. Although not shown, cheap day fares had appeared by the mid-1920s since when reduced price and special offer fares for off-peak travellers have been a regular feature. Workmen's tickets were never available from Welwyn North in GNR days and early morning returns were withdrawn in January 1962.

The general pattern of fares is set out in Table 13.3. For about 65 years (1850 to 1915), and probably throughout the period up to amalgamation (1923), first class fares fell slightly and third class fares remained little changed. For some years thereafter the differentials between the cost of first and third class travel, and to a lesser extent between ordinary single and return fares, were subject to variation. Until 1986 British Railways consistently set first class fares at 1½ times the second class rate. From 1986, however, the price of first class season tickets has been calculated on a new formula based on the price of a second class ticket plus a supplement which is a multiple of the difference between the first and second class single fares.

Significant increases first occurred during the operation of the line by the LNER (1923 to 1947). These were modest when compared with the acceleration in fare increases that took place between 1960 and 1986. The calculations in Table 13.4 show that

the largest increases have been in the price of season tickets. As the commuter business, whereby customers buy season tickets for daily travel to and from work, has increased, so the saving offered against buying ordinary return tickets has fallen. The effect of this is that in the eighty years to 1986, season ticket price rises were double those for ordinary fares.

A factor peculiar to the Great Northern line has been several above-average fare rises to meet the cost of the improved post-electrification service. This is illustrated in Table 13.5 which provides a comparison of the cost of rail travel between Peterborough, Welwyn North, Woking and London.

13.2 Tickets

The familiar railway Booking Office took its name from the days of stage coach travel when intending passengers attended at the office and their travel requirements were entered in a book, whereupon the clerk would write a manifest or waybill which the coach guard would use to prepare his passenger list.

Written tickets continued to be issued by the early railways but with considerable foresight Thomas Edmondson, whilst Station Master at Milton (now Brampton) on the Newcastle and Carlisle Railway in the late 1830s, devised the first card railway ticket. Later pre-printed and serially numbered, these became

TABLE 13.5 *Comparative costs of travel to London in June 1986*

Station	Miles to London	2nd class fare to London		Cost of travel per mile		Number of trains from London 1700–1800	Fastest journey speed (mph)
		Ordinary single	Annual season	Ordinary single	Annual season		
		£	£	p	£		
Peterborough	76¼	10.70	1640	14.0	21.51	3	95.3
Welwyn North	22	3.20	980	14.5	44.55	3	45.5
Woking	24¼	3.10	936	12.8	38.60	18	56.0

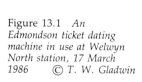

Figure 13.1 *An Edmondson ticket dating machine in use at Welwyn North station, 17 March 1986* © *T. W. Gladwin*

Plate 8   *A selection of GNR, LNER and BR tickets covering the period 1904 to 1986:*
(C1) 1904 GNR Third class single, Cambridge to Kings Cross: fare 4s 7½d; (A1)
1912 GNR First class single, Kings Cross to Market Weighton: fare 27s 11d; (B1)
1921 GNR Second class single, Finsbury Park to Canonbury; (A2) 1939 LNER
Third class single, Kings Cross to Welwyn North: fare 2s 11d; (B2) 1939 LNER Third
class child single, Kings Cross to Welwyn North: fare 1s 5d; (C2) 1952 BR (E),
LNER-style, Third class day return Welwyn North to Welwyn Garden City: fare 6d;

(A4) 1953 BR (E), Third class day return excess fare Welwyn North to Welwyn Garden
City: amount 6d. Issued at Welwyn Garden City; (B3) 1979 BR, Second class day
return Welwyn (North) to Stevenage. Note brackets to the word 'North'; (C3) 1985
BR First Class half rate return Welwyn North to London (K/X) or Moorgate; (A3)
1986 BR Second class cheap day half rate return, Welwyn North to any London
Transport station in Zones 1 and 2. Note mis-spelling of Moorgate; (B4) 1986 BR
Platform ticket, Welwyn North; (C4) 1986 BR Car parking ticket, Welwyn North

© *T. W. Gladwin*

standard on all British as well as many foreign railways. Even the dimensions remained the same worldwide. Edmondson subsequently designed and produced ticket date-stamping machines, one of which, the inked ribbon, as distinct from the inked pad, type is still in use in 1986 at Welwyn North station.

A wide variety of tickets would have been maintained at Welwyn station. These were stored in racks (*see* Figure 13.2), also designed by Edmondson, for many more types of traffic than at present. From the point of view of those who study the history of railway tickets it is fortunate that electronic ticket-issuing and -dating equipment has not yet been installed. Thus the Edmondson machine may still be available for its 50 000th day of use in June 1987! Plate 8 includes various types of tickets issued to and from Welwyn North by the LNER and BR. For the sake of completeness earlier examples of GNR tickets are also illustrated, although none relate to Welwyn. Sadly not one example has been traced of a ticket issued from or to 'Welwyn' and bearing that title, which was its name before it was changed to 'Welwyn North' with the opening of the new Welwyn Garden City station in 1926.

The GNRs tickets were standardised on white cards for first class, mauve/red for second class, and blue for third class. Variations included overprinted stripes or letters to denote travel through to other companies' lines. Second class was progressively abolished. By July 1886 it remained only on Anglo–Scottish services and local trains in the London area. It was withdrawn from the former on 1 July 1892 and, as mentioned earlier, from local trains to and from stations north of New Barnet in 1891. After the grouping of railways on 1 January 1923, the LNER continued the use of white cards for first class and introduced blue for second class and green for third class. The remaining second class facilities on former GN lines were withdrawn in 1942. The green colour was retained when third class was reclassified second class on 3 June 1956.

To the present day (May 1986) white cards have continued to be issued for first class tickets and have also been adopted for all second class single and return ordinary (full fare) tickets.

Figure 13.2 *The Edmondson card railway ticket issuing rack at Welwyn North station on 17 March 1986* © T. W. Gladwin

All second class day return tickets are printed on red cards, some of which are designed to be torn in half on completion of the outward journey. Others, wholly retained throughout both outward and return journey, bear the additional words 'and back'. First class day returns were abolished on 16 May 1983.

Season tickets have varied over the years. Unfortunately few early examples survive, as the issuing company went to

Figure 13.3 *An unmodified GNR ticket office at Welwyn North station, 17 March 1986* © T. W. Gladwin

considerable trouble to collect expired seasons. BR have variously used red and green cardboard with rounded corners. The range was considerably reduced when London Transport adopted a zonal fares system on 4 October 1981. Since about 1977 the design of monthly second class tickets has been of red print on a white rectangular card with 'British Rail' closely printed in multiple over the entire surface. There is also space for the number of a photocard which has to be produced by the ticket holder. Photocards were introduced to ensure that a season ticket was used solely by the person to whom it had been issued. This enabled the practice of stamping 'W' on tickets issued to women to be discontinued.

As with monthly season tickets, a white card with red security printing of 'British Rail' and red printing of the substantive details is used for the first class season tickets to 'Kings Cross or Moorgate'. The choice of London termini was introduced with the electrification to Moorgate in 1976. The duration of such tickets, in months and days, is entered in ink. First class annual season tickets take the form of a white card printed in blue and security-overprinted with the words 'BR Annual' in red. The second class annual season ticket is similar but the security printing is in blue. Other permutations of blue and red occur on other season tickets. In contrast the first class 7-day All-Zones Capitalcard is printed in brown on a white card with no security printing.

Daily and period car parking tickets are printed greenish-yellow Edmondson cards with space for the vehicle registration number. In 1986 the period ticket is to be replaced by a larger white card.

Platform tickets, as still issued in 1986, are printed in black on a white Edmondson card overprinted with a green diamond in the centre.

Over the years the destinations for which pre-printed tickets

are available have been considerably reduced. Stocks in the main are confined to those places to which a reasonable passenger demand could be expected, such as Kings Cross, Welwyn Garden City, other stations served by the electric units, and Cambridge. It is particularly interesting to note that second class single tickets of the last green issue are still being issued, in June 1986, for journeys from Welwyn North to Brookmans Park, New Barnet and Hornsey/Wood Green. Wood Green was renamed Alexandra Palace in May 1982! Other Edmondson card issues are in stock for privilege, that is reduced-rate, tickets for railway staff, bicycle tickets, travel to Gatwick and Heathrow airports, and for special promotions. For other destinations the booking clerk prepares a paper ticket, with carbons forming the return half, on the airline principle, and a copy retained for accounting purposes. These are supplied in pads of serially-numbered blanks printed in red on yellow paper for destinations on BR, and in green on yellow for destinations on London Transport railways.

13.3 Luggage labels

Although these are not strictly within the purview of 'fares and tickets' it is worth commenting on the distinctive luggage labels which were once extensively used on the railways. When the conveyance of parcels and personal luggage was significant each station maintained a rack of luggage labels for each destination on its own system and often to many on other lines where the value of traffic justified printing and holding such a stock. These labels were affixed to luggage and parcels to be placed in the luggage vans of passenger trains and facilitated off-loading by the guard. Figure 13.4 illustrates a luggage label issued from a GNR station to Welwyn.

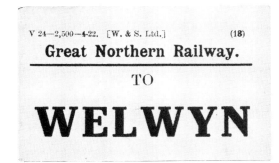

Figure 13.4 *A GNR luggage label*
Courtesy of D. E. White

Chapter 14

Population and Passengers

New residents often ask how it is that a small rural community like Digswell came to benefit from a main line railway service. The answer is illustrated by a study of the population figures provided in Table 14.1. In 1851, a year after the opening of the line and a year for which reliable population figures exist, only Hatfield, Hitchin and Royston of the Great Northern lineside towns and villages in present-day Hertfordshire had larger populations than Welwyn. Even Barnet, now part of Greater London and comprising East Barnet and Chipping Barnet, was only slightly larger. Welwyn station, now Welwyn North, was therefore built to serve Welwyn, then a relatively major area of population. Indeed, had the original plan for a route via Kimpton and Kings Walden been adopted, Welwyn station would have been built in Welwyn village. In that event Digswell would never have had a main line railway and the village would almost certainly be a very different place from what it is today.

The subsequent growth of the lineside towns and villages is well illustrated by Table 14.1. The figures for Digswell from 1851 to 1951 refer to the Parish of Digswell, the majority of the population living north of what is now the B1000, Welwyn to Hertford, road or in the area known as Digswell Water and around Digswell House. The figures for 1971 and 1981 are those for the area of Digswell and Harmer Green north of the B1000 road only. The area known as Digswell Water had 569 residents in 1981 and is now treated as part of the Haldens Ward of Welwyn Garden City for national census of population purposes.

Information on the numbers of passengers travelling to and from Welwyn North has been hard to find. In 1925, 136 season tickets were issued at Welwyn North. This had increased to 174 in 1929. It is not clear whether or not the figure refers to the number of season ticket holders or whether, for example, a passenger buying four quarterly tickets counts as four in the figures given. In 1969 and again in 1979 the number of peak

TABLE 14.1 *Population ('000s) of towns and villages along the Great Northern Line in Hertfordshire 1851–1981*

Town/Village	Date station opened	1851	1891	1901	1911	1921	1931	1951	1961	1971	1981
Potters Bar	1850	1.9	2.6E	2.7	2.8	3.1	5.7	17.2	23.4	24.6	23.2
Hatfield	1850	3.8	4.3	4.8	5.3	5.7	6.6	13.8	21.0	26.0	25.3
Welwyn Garden City[b]	1926	—	0.2	0.4	0.6	0.9	8.7	18.3	35.2	40.4	40.5
Welwyn[a]	1850	2.2	2.1	2.2	2.3	2.5	3.7	5.4	6.9	8.4	8.7
Knebworth	1884	0.3	0.4	0.5	1.3	1.6	2.2	2.7	3.0	3.5	3.9
Stevenage	1850	2.1	3.3	4.0	4.9	5.1	5.5	6.6	43.0	67.1	74.4
Hitchin	1850	7.1	8.9	10.4	12.5	13.5	14.4	20.0	24.3	28.7	30.3
Letchworth	1905	—	0.1	0.3	5.3	10.3	14.7	20.3	25.6	30.9	31.8
Baldock	1850	1.9	2.2	2.1	2.1	2.5	3.2	6.0	6.7	6.3	6.7
Ashwell	1850	1.4	1.6	1.3	1.3	1.2	1.3	1.3	1.3	1.4	1.6
Royston	1850	3.5	3.3	3.5	4.0	3.8	3.9	4.7	6.2	8.3	11.8
Digswell (Actual population)		239	240	242	401	423	644	740	?	1307	1413

NOTES: E Estimated
(a) Population given is for Ayot St Lawrence, Ayot St Peter, Digswell (which includes Harmer Green), Mardley Heath, Oaklands, Welwyn and Woolmer Green. In 1901 some 70 per cent of population lived in Welwyn village and in 1981 just under 42 per cent.
(b) A halt existed prior to 1926 but did not give access to London or main-line services.
(c) Brookmans Park Station, not shown, opened in 1926. By 1951 population was about 1900.

period (0700–0959) passengers joining trains at Welwyn North was 280. This had risen to 358 by 1982. This compares with peak period boarding numbers of 1609 at Potters Bar, 548 at Brookmans Park, 1012 at Hatfield, 1385 at Welwyn Garden City, 285 at Knebworth, 1461 at Stevenage, 1223 at Hitchin, 811 at Letchworth, 130 at Baldock, 106 at Ashwell and 908 at Royston. Thus it seems that the growth in passenger traffic to and from Welwyn North has been much smaller than at most other Hertfordshire stations on the Great Northern line.

None the less, first class travel remains buoyant, with about eighteen annual season ticket holders, not counting railway staff. Indeed, British Rail believe that the proportion of passengers travelling first class is higher at Welwyn North than at any other Kings Cross suburban station. The new Class 317 units (referred to in Chapter 10) on this line continue to provide two-class accommodation, although the London–Bedford Class 317 units run as second class only.

A passenger count made by British Railways at Welwyn North in November 1983 showed a daily (Monday to Friday) average of 73 passengers boarding northbound trains and 532 passengers boarding southbound trains. The six most popular departures from Welwyn North were all southbound and were 0814 (110 passengers boarding), 0750 (107), 0727 (74), 0840 fast (64), 0830 (57) and 0657 (29). The most popular northbound departure was the 0804 (12). As might be expected, the six most popular arrivals at Welwyn North were all northbound evening trains and were the 1810 ex-Kings Cross (89 passengers alighting), 1733 (58), 1840 (56), 1748 (53), 1708 (43) and 1640 (30). A peak period passenger count made by the authors at Welwyn North in May 1985 found passengers joining southbound trains as follows: 0750 (44 passengers boarding), 0801 (91), 0813 (61), 0830 (68), and 0839 (24). The figures for the then new fast 0801, and the decelerated 0839 compared with the fast 0840 of 1983, show the popularity of fast trains. There were 140 000 rail passenger journeys from London to Welwyn North compared with 138 000 from London to Edinburgh in 1983.

Survey work carried out by Hertfordshire County Council in 1982 found that 8 per cent of all journeys to work by Hertfordshire residents are made by train. Three quarters of all rail journeys from the county are journeys to work, mostly in central London. Between 1969 and 1982 the number of peak period passengers joining trains on the Great Northern line increased from 8010 to 11 700. The 358 joining at Welwyn North represents 3 per cent of this total. About 57 per cent of peak-period travellers on the Great Northern line have season tickets.

Chapter 15

The Cowper Arms

The Cowper Arms is situated on the west side of the East Coast Main Line adjacent to Welwyn North station at the northern end of Digswell Viaduct. The public house was built about 1850 by, it is believed, the same gangs of navvies that built the viaduct and tunnels, as the nearest drinking house was then at Burnham Green some distance away. It is evident that The Cowper Arms was originally known as 'The Railway Inn' or 'The Railway Arms'. It was built on the estate of Lord Cowper and eventually took the name of its landlord. The original part of the building remains virtually unaltered since these early days. However, the function of each room has varied as requirements have changed with the times and to fit in with the purposes of three extensions to the premises. The first of these was in about 1900 when a 'snug' bar was added. In the 1920s a more ambitious project added three more bedrooms and a bathroom (*see* Figure 15.2), and in 1965 the total ground area of the public house was more than doubled when a new lounge bar and restaurant was built along its west side. Recognising the increasing use and numbers of cars, fifty parking spaces were provided at the same time. Unfortunately this work meant the loss of the ornate rockeries and the sunken garden that had been a valued part of Digswell's history.

The Cowper Arms was for many years an hotel with four bedrooms owned by Home Counties P.H. Trust Ltd. In its early days the rooms were let with all modern conveniences, namely a washstand with a jug of cold water and a chamber pot! Facilities also included a cycle store and stables. By the early 1950s the cost of a week's stay in Digswell had risen to just under £7 for which a guest received breakfast, lunch (three courses), afternoon tea, dinner (also three courses) and garaging facilities. During the period when The Cowper Arms was an hotel some notorious people were recorded as having visited or stayed there. These included the murderer Dr Crippen, who stayed in Bedroom No 1. Many show business personalities travelled to Digswell during the two world wars for a short break from London and the bombing. Visitors to Digswell Park Conference House (Digswell House) sometimes extended their stay in the village with a few days in residence at The Cowper Arms. Paul Robeson, the singer, is known to have stayed there and Hugh Gaitskell to have at least visited it.

The Cowper Arms lost its hotel status in 1958 when a partnership between two local breweries (Whitbreads and McMullens) purchased the house from Trust Houses Ltd. This partnership ended in 1983 when McMullen & Sons Ltd of Hertford became the sole owner.

The connection between The Cowper Arms and the railway goes back to the very beginnings of the railway and it could truly be said that they serve one another.

Figure 15.1 *The Cowper Arms Hotel, Digswell 1915* *Courtesy of C. Williams*

Figure 15.2   *The Cowper Arms Hotel in the 1920s*   *Courtesy of C. Williams*

Following the accident in Welwyn North Tunnel on 9 June 1866 (*see* Chapter 12) the bodies of Joseph Wray (guard) and John Rawlins were laid in The Cowper Arms and the inquest held in the bar. *The Times* report of the incident referred to 'The Railway Arms Inn' whilst other papers called it 'The Cowper Arms'.

On 17 June 1935 the inspector inquiring into the accident at Welwyn Garden City, when Class K3 No 4009 ran into the rear of a Kings Cross to Newcastle train, stayed at The Cowper Arms in order to inspect the locomotive which had been stored since the accident in Welwyn North sidings.

In the past The Cowper Arms offered comfortable and quiet accommodation to travellers and those seeking a time in the country. Today it is still a thriving public house serving Digswell village, Welwyn and the surrounding districts and is still the haunt of off-duty railway operating and maintenance staff, and many passengers.

Figure 15.3   *The Cowper Arms, Digswell 1986*   © *T. W. Gladwin*

Chapter 16

Today and Tomorrow

Throughout the years since its opening in 1850 Welwyn station, renamed Welwyn North in 1926, has maintained its position in catering for rail traffic from a wide catchment area in spite of the supplementary services available from Welwyn Garden City station, which, as its name suggests, primarily serves the country's second garden city. There have been many changes. In particular, technical advances have resulted in faster and more frequent train services being available to the greatly increased population. (*See* Chapter 14.) By May 1986 outer suburban trains (Class 312 units) which served the two stations at Welwyn ran at up to 90 mph between stops, and the inner suburban trains (Class 313 units) from Welwyn Garden City to Moorgate at up to 75 mph between stations north of Finsbury Park. New Class 317/2 units, introduced on the outer suburban services in 1986, are intended to run at up to 100 mph between stops. The fast outer suburban services connect at Stevenage with HST 125 mph trains to and from West Yorkshire, North East England and Scotland and thereby provide Welwyn with services at least as good as, if not better than, anywhere else of its size in the country. This is particularly remarkable for a town with Welwyn's rural position relative to London. The equipment, including motive power, rolling stock and signalling, is undoubtedly capable of providing the most efficient and reliable services.

By 1986 the services available at the two Welwyn stations have become largely confined to passenger traffic, although at Welwyn Garden City there is a privately operated goods yard, opened in 1986, and other limited parcels facilities remain. Which station people choose to use depends not just on which they live closer to. Those living within walking distance of one or other of the two stations naturally tend to use it, but residents in the outlying villages are influenced by the ease of car parking.

Thus, for example, not all commuters from Welwyn or Wheathampstead necessarily use Welwyn North. Some, perhaps those travelling by the earlier departures when parking space is readily available, use Welwyn Garden City whilst others travel from Hatfield or even St Albans or Harpenden. Free parking still attracts a minority to park in the quieter residential roads at Digswell in order to travel from Welwyn North.

British Railways view commuters as captive customers and do not deny that this is reflected in fare calculations. However, few low-paid employees now commute daily to London, the days of cheap early morning workmen's tickets having long disappeared. However, rises in the earnings of those who continue to work in London have tended to keep pace with increases in fares. This has contributed to stabilising the volume of commuter traffic.

Forecasts of future passenger patterns and numbers are difficult to make. Uncertain factors include employment trends, as new technology reduces the need for the large commercial and financial institutions to employ vast numbers of clerical staff, and the movement towards flexible working times, shorter working weeks and increased leisure. There has also been a tendency for businesses that do not need to be situated in or close to the City of London or the revitalised dockland areas to decentralise their administrative organisations away from London.

Any further shift of passengers from rail to road is also difficult to foresee. As is evident from the congestions on the A1(M), M1 and M25, estimates of motorway use, particularly during the rush-hour periods, have been lamentably deficient. Road travel therefore remains an unattractive option for many Hertfordshire passengers. Most villages within the catchment area of the two Welwyn stations are subject to infilling or even expansion, with further residential development that might be expected to increase the travelling population, particularly as local industry has reduced its manpower requirements. Present policies, however, seek to increase the number of small businesses in Welwyn Hatfield providing jobs for local people. In the short term there seems to be only a low probability of any significant change in the patterns of commuter travel, and the present general level of rush hour services is therefore likely to continue. Services may, however, become faster in response to competitive pressures from other modes of transport and also to the operational requirements of the faster main line services which are expected following the electrification of the lines to Leeds and Scotland.

Most travel for leisure purposes is made during the off-peak periods outside the rush hours when lower fares apply. More leisure could significantly increase the utilisation of services during the slack periods of the day. In anticipation of this, in May 1986, outer suburban off peak services between Kings Cross and Letchworth/Royston began calling at Alexandra Palace to allow access to the leisure complex being developed by the local authority. This station is thus served by two fast outer suburban and three 'all stations' Welwyn Garden City inner suburban trains each hour off peak in each direction on weekdays. The introduction of new Class 317/2 four-car electric driver-only-operated units on the outer suburban trains from May 1986 mitigates the extra time involved in making this additional stop.

On 3 November 1986 one of the outer suburban services in each direction is to be extended to Huntingdon and in May 1987 Peterborough will be served by the outer suburban trains using the Class 317/2 units, and this is expected to satisfy demand for the next decade. The electrification to Peterborough is the first stage of the electrification of the main line from Kings Cross to Leeds and Edinburgh.

No announcements have been made regarding any possible replacement of the Class 313 inner suburban units which should be capable of coping with this traffic for several more years.

British Railways have recently announced that the line through Snow Hill tunnel is to be re-opened and some trains from Bedford will then run via Kentish Town, Farringdon and Blackfriars to East Croydon. Gauging tests have also been carried out as part of a feasibility study into reinstating services along the small radius curves from Kings Cross towards Farringdon. Perhaps, therefore, Welwyn North passengers will be able one day to travel direct to Blackfriars, Elephant & Castle, Croydon, and beyond into the depths of Kent, Surrey and Sussex.

Appendix A
Chronological History of the Opening and Closing of Great Northern Lines and Stations in Hertfordshire

1 The Main Line: Maiden Lane and Kings Cross to Hitchin

1850	The formal public opening of the line from Maiden Lane to Peterborough took place on 7 August. Intermediate stations between Barnet and Hitchin were Potter's Bar & South Mimms* (then in Middlesex), Hatfield, Welwyn, and Stevenage.
1852	Kings Cross station and the section of line from there to Maiden Lane opened on 14 October.
1873	Oakleigh Park* station (then in Hertfordshire), opened on 4 December.
1884	Knebworth station opened on 1 February. Barnet renamed New Barnet*.
1885	Hadley Wood station (Middlesex) opened on 1 May.
1926	Brookmans Park station opened on 19 July. Welwyn Garden City station, replacing platforms on the Dunstable and Hertford branch lines, formally opened on 5 October although trains started using the station on 20 September. Welwyn station renamed Welwyn North.
1973	New station opened at Stevenage on 23 July on a site south of the former station which closed on the same day.
1986	Welham Green station opened on 29 September.

2 The Royston and Hitchin Line

1846	Royston and Hitchin Railway Bill received the Royal Assent on 16 July.
1848	Parliament approved extension from Royston to Cambridge.
1850	GNR obtained lease of the line from Hitchin to Shepreth on 1 August. The section of the line from Hitchin to Royston opened on 21 October with two intermediate stations at Baldock, and Ashwell & Morden.
1866	The GNRs through services from Kings Cross to Cambridge started on 1 April.
1905	A halt was opened at Letchworth on 15 April.
1913	The present passenger station, replacing the halt, was opened at Letchworth on 18 May.

* As a result of boundary changes at 1 April 1965, New Barnet and Oakleigh Park became part of the London Borough of Barnet and Potters Bar part of Hertfordshire.

1978	Through passenger services from Kings Cross to Cambridge withdrawn in February upon electrification of the line to Royston.

3 The Hertford Loop: Wood Green to Langley Junction

1871	Branch from Wood Green to Enfield (Middlesex) opened on 1 April.
1910	Enfield to Cuffley section opened on 4 April with intermediate stations at Gordon Hill and Crews Hill. The new section started from a point south of the original terminus at Enfield which was then closed. The new station at Enfield was later renamed Enfield Chase.
1918	A single line from Cuffley to Langley Junction was opened to goods traffic in March.
1920	Widening of the Cuffley to Langley Junction section to two tracks completed in November.
1924	Passenger services commenced running north of Cuffley to and from Stevenage via Langley Junction on 2 June. Intermediate stations opened at Bayford, Hertford North, Stapleford and Watton-at-Stone. The Welwyn to Hertford branch connected at the same time to allow trains to terminate at Hertford North and Hertford Cowbridge closed.
1939	Passenger services between Hertford North and Stevenage (Langley Junction) withdrawn on 11 September. Stapleford and Watton-at-Stone stations closed.
1962	Passenger services between Hertford North and Stevenage (Langley Junction) restored on 5 March.
1982	Watton-at-Stone station re-opened on 17 May.

4 The Hatfield and St Albans Branch

1865	The single line branch Hatfield & St Albans Railway (6 miles) opened on 16 October under GNR operation.
1866	Intermediate station opened at Springfield on 1 February. GNR trains started running through to the LNWRs Abbey station on 1 November.
1879	Springfield station renamed Smallford on 10 October.
1883	Act of Parliament vested the Hatfield & St Albans Railway in the GNR from 1 November.

1890	Sanders siding, also known as Sanders and Salvation Army siding, opened. Trains stopped there in daytime on request only at a small passenger platform.
1899	Halt opened at Hill End in October.
1910	Halt opened at Nast Hyde on 1 February.
1939	Passenger services withdrawn from September to December.
1942	Halt opened at Lemsford Road (Hatfield) on 1 August.
1951	Line closed on 1 October.

5 The High Barnet Branch: Finchley to High Barnet

1872	The Finchley to High Barnet branch opened on 1 April. Two stations, Totteridge & Whetstone and High Barnet, were then in Hertfordshire.
1940	The branch was electrified and tube trains replaced steam on 14 April when ownership was transferred to the London Passenger Transport Board.

6 The Hertford and Welwyn Branch

1854	The Hertford & Welwyn Junction Railway incorporated on 3 July.
1858	GNR commenced operation of passenger services between Hertford Cowbridge and Welwyn Junction on 1 March. Intermediate stations were at Cole Green and Hertingfordbury.
	Hertford & Welwyn Junction and Luton, Dunstable and Welwyn Railway companies amalgamated on 28 June to form the Hertford, Luton & Dunstable Railway.
1860	Platform at Welwyn Junction closed on 1 September and subsequently removed.
1861	The Hertford, Luton & Dunstable Railway was vested in the GNR by an Act of 12 June.
1905	Temporary halts at Hatfield Hyde and Attimore closed on 1 July.
1917	A new platform for workmen erected at Welwyn Junction, now Welwyn Garden City. Passenger services were never timetabled to call there. (Cockman 1983 gives the date of the new platform as 1 September 1920. This latter is close to the date of 16 August 1920 when the platform named Welwyn Garden City on the Luton & Dunstable Branch was opened to passenger services.)
1924	Section from Hertford North to Hertford Cowbridge closed to passenger traffic on 2 June when Hertford North became the terminus.

1926	Passenger services started calling at the new Welwyn Garden City station on 20 September.
1951	Passenger services withdrawn from the branch on 18 June.
1966	Goods services to Hertford Cowbridge withdrawn on 23 May and the line closed. Trains conveying Greater London Council rubbish to tips at Holwell Hyde and Cole Green ceased one month earlier.

7 The Luton and Dunstable Branch

1855	The Luton, Dunstable & Welwyn Junction Railway was incorporated on 16 July.
1858	Freight services between Luton and Dunstable (LNWR) commenced on 5 April.
	Passenger services over the same section commenced on 3 May.
	The Luton, Dunstable & Welwyn Junction and the Hertford & Welwyn Junction railway companies amalgamated to form the Hertford, Luton & Dunstable Railway on 28 June.
1860	The single line section from Welwyn Junction to Luton opened on 1 September. All services were operated by the GNR from the outset. Intermediate stations were at New Mill End, Harpenden and Wheathampstead.
1861	The Hertford, Luton & Dunstable Railway was vested in the GNR by an Act of 12 June.
1877	Ayott St Peter station opened on 2 July.
1878	Ayott St Peter station renamed Ayot.
1898	New Mill End became Luton Hoo for New Mill End.
1917	A new platform for workmen erected on the branch at Welwyn (north of the present Welwyn Garden City station).
1920	On 16 August passenger services commenced calling at the platform built in 1917 and named Welwyn Garden City.
1926	Passenger services started calling at the new Welwyn Garden City station on 20 September when the platform constructed in 1917 was closed.
1965	Passenger services withdrawn from the branch on 24 April.
1966	Following installation of a connection between the Midland main-line and Luton East, the section between Luton (Vauxhall Ground Frame) and Blackbridge Sidings (Wheathampstead) was closed.
1970	Rubbish trains from Ashburton Grove (Finsbury Park) to Blackbridge Tip ceased in October and the last section of the branch from Welwyn Garden City closed.

Appendix B1

Great Northern Railway Timetable for August 1852

August.] MAIN LINE.—LONDON to YORK, via Grantham and Newark. [1852.

DOWN.

Miles	STATIONS.						WEEK DAYS.										SUNDAYS.		
		1	2	3	4	5	6	7	8	9	10	11	12	13	14	1	2	3

Stations as far as York.

Miles	Station
0	LONDON, dep. King's Cross
4	Hornsey
6½	Colney Hatch and Southgate
9½	BARNET
12½	Potter's Bar and South Mims
17½	HATFIELD for St. Alban's and Luton
22	Welwyn
28½	Stevenage
32	HITCHIN
37	Arlsey and Shefford Road
41	BIGGLESWADE
44	Sandy for Bedford & Potton
51½	ST. NEOTS (by Bedfd. ch.)
55½	Offord
59	HUNTINGDON for St. Ives
69¼	Holme
76½	PETERBOROUGH ..... arrival
	Ditto ..... departure
84½	Tallington for STAMFORD
88⅜	Essendine
92	Little Bytham
97	CORBY
102½	Great Ponton
105¼	GRANTHAM, for Nottingham
128	NOTTINGHAM ..... arrival
	Ditto ..... departure

Miles	Station
111¼	Hougham and Marston
115¼	Clayyole
120	NEWARK
126¼	Carlton
131½	TUXFORD
138½	RETFORD ..... arrival
	Ditto ..... departure
142	Sutton
144	Ranskill
146	Scrooby
148	BAWTRY
151¾	Rossington
156½	DONCASTER ..... arrival
	Ditto ..... departure
173¾	Barnsley
158¼	Arksey and Stockbridge
162¼	Askern
166¼	Norton
166¾	Womersley
171	KNOTTINGLEY Junc. ..ar
	Ditto ..... departure
186½	LEEDS ..... arrival
181½	BRADFORD (Coach & Rail)
	WAKEFIELD ..... arrival
	Burton Salmon
176	Milford Junction for HULL
	HULL, viâ Milford .. arrival
178	Sherborne ..... departure
180	Church Fenton for Harrogate
198½	HARROGATE ..... arrival
182	Ulleskelf ..... departure
183½	Bolton Percy
187	Copmanthorpe
191	YORK ..... arrival

** ** Down Trains 3 and 7 will call at Burton Salmon with London Passengers only.

** * This No. 12 Down Train will stop at Bawtry, to put down First Class Passengers from London.

NOTE: The trains marked 'Parly' were trains which by Parliamentary law had to call at all stations, average at least 12 mph, and charge not more than 1d (0.4p) per mile third class.

Extract from the Great Northern Railway Timetable Commencing 28 July 1887

SUBURBAN AND CITY TRAINS TO LONDON.—Week days.—UP.

UP

The table lists the following stations (reading down the left-hand column), with numerous train times across the columns (a.m.):

- CAMBRIDGE .... dep.
- HITCHIN .... dep.
- Stevenage
- Knebworth
- Welwyn
- LUTON
- DUNSTABLE (Chrch St.) ... dep.
- Do.
- LUTON .... arr.
- HERTFORD .... arr.
- Do. .... dep.
- ST. ALBANS (G.N.) .... arr
- Do.
- HATFIELD .... dep.
- Potters Bar
- Hadley Wood
- New Barnet
- Oakleigh Park
- New Southgate
- ENFIELD .... dep.
- Winchmore Hill
- Palmers Gn. & S'gate
- Bowes Park
- Wood Green (Alex. Park).
- Hornsey
- Harringay
- EDGWARE .... dep.
- Mill Hill
- HIGH BARNET
- Totteridge & Whetstone
- Woodside Park
- Finchley
- East Finchley
- ALEXANDRA PAL
- Muswell Hill
- HIGHGATE
- Crouch End
- Stroud Green
- Finsbury Park .... dep.
- Canonbury
- Mildmay Park
- Dalston Junction
- Haggerston
- Shoreditch
- BROAD STREET
- Holloway .... dep.
- York Road (King's Cross) ... dep
- KING'S CROSS (Term.) .... arr
- King's Cross (Metrop.)
- Farringdon
- Aldersgate
- MOORGATE
- Aldersgate .... dep.
- Farringdon
- Snow Hill .... arr
- LUDGATE HILL
- CANNON STREET
- LONDON BRIDGE
- Spa Road .... dep.
- New Cross
- St. John's
- Lewisham Junction
- BLACKHEATH
- Charlton Junction
- WOOLWICH (D'yd) .... arr.
- (Arsenal.)
- Boro' Road .... dep.
- Elephant & Castle
- Walworth Road
- Camberwell New Rd.
- Loughboro' Jun.
- Brixton
- CRYSTAL PAL. (H.L.) .... arr
- Clapham .... arr.
- Wandsworth Road
- Battersea Park
- Grosvenor Road
- VICTORIA

NOTES (bottom of table): Holders of Workmen's tickets may return from Moorgate Street on any week day by any train after 12.0 noon. They are not allowed to travel in any but 3rd class carriages. The tickets are only available on the day of issue and by the specified trains. * Stops to take up or leave passengers when required. Passengers wishing to alight must give notice to the guard at the preceding station. A Passengers to stations Snow Hill to Victoria inclusive change carriages at Aldersgate Street, B Passengers to stations, Snow Hill to Victoria inclusive, change carriages at Farringdon street. E Stops at Hitchin when required to take up passengers for London only. ¶ Passengers are not booked from Snow Hill or Ludgate Hill to South Eastern stations.

NOTES: Through and connecting trains are not clearly distinguishable. The timetable includes services beyond Kings Cross since the railways at that time conveyed passengers to locations all over inner London later served by the Underground.

Appendix B3

Extract from one of the last Great Northern Railway Timetables Commencing 3 October 1921

SUBURBAN AND CITY.

WEEK DAYS.   **FROM LONDON.**

Leaves King's X Platform		14	11	14	13	14	13	12	14	11	12		12		13		13	12	13		
	p.m.	p.m.	p.m.	p.m.	p.m.	p.m.	p.m.	p.m.	p.m.	p.m.	p.m.	p.m.	p.m.	p.m.	p.m.	p.m.	p.m.	p.m.	p.m.	p.m.	p.m.
MOORGATE ... dep.		12 26		12 34		12 40		12 47			12 55			1 3			1 13		1 19	
Aldersgate		12 28		12 36		12 42		12 49			12 57			1 5			1 15		1 21	
Farringdon		12 30		12 38		12 44		12 51			12 59			1 11			1 17		1 23	
King's X (Metropolitan)		12 34		12 42		12 48		12 55			1 3			1 11			1 21		1 27	
KING'S X (G N)	J	12 37	12 40	12 45	12 45	12 52	12 58	1 2	12 50	1 5	1 6	G	1 11	1 16	J	1 20	1 23	1 27	J
BROAD STREET	12 25				12 34			1 10				1 11			1 18		1 26	
Shoreditch	12 9				12 36			1 5				1 9			1 20		1 24	
Haggerston	12 12				12 39		12 57			1 12				1 27	
Dalston Junction	12 25				12 41		1 9				1 17			1 25		1 31	
Mildmay Park	12 27				12 43		1 11				1 27			1 29	
Canonbury	12 29				12 45		1 13				1 21			1 34	
FINSBURY PARK ... arr.	12 33	12 42		12 50	12 50 12 57	1 3	1 10	1 11	1 12		1 16 1 19	1 21 1 22	1 25 1 25	1 29 1 32	1 33	1 36 1 38
" " ... dep.	12 35	12 37 12 43		12 51 12 51 12 51	12 54 12 59	1 2 1 4	1 6 1 6	1 11 1 12 1 13	1 14	1 17 1 18	1 18 1 20	1 21 1 23	1 26 1 26 1 26	1 26	1 30 1 34	1 35	1 39 1 39
Stroud Green		12 40		12 54 12 57	12 58	1 5	1 9		1 17 1 21		1 29		1 29	1 33 1 37		1 42
Crouch End		12 43		12 57	1 1	1 8	1 12		1 20 1 24		1 32		1 30	1 37		1 45
Highgate		12 47		1 1	1 6	1 12	1 16		1 24 1 25		1 36		1 36	1 40 1 44		1 49
Cranley Gardens				1 4		1 15	1 19		1 31					1 43		1 52
Muswell Hill				1 6		1 17	1 21		1 33					1 45		1 54
ALEXANDRA PALACE ... arr.				1 8		1 19	1 23		1 36					1 47		1 56
East Finchley ... dep.	12 46	12 53			1 10				1 28		1 39		1 30	1 48	
Finchley (Church End)	12 51	12 58			1 15				1 32		1 44		1 44	1 52	
Finchley (Church End)	12 55	12 58				1 25							1 55	
Mill Hill (for Mill Hill Bks.)	12 58	1 0				1 28							1 58	
The Hale (for Mill Hill)	1 2					1 32							2 2	
EDGWARE	1 5					1 35							2 5	
Woodside Pk. (for N. Fn'ly) dep.	12 55	1 3			1 19					1 48		1 48	1 56	
Totteridge	12 58	1 6			1 22					1 51		1 51	1 59	
HIGH BARNET ... arr.	1 2	1 10			1 26					1 55		1 55	2 3	
Harringay ... dep.		12 46		12 54 12 54	1 2	1 9 1 9	1 15 1 16		1 24 1 26	1 29 1 29	1 30	1 38	1 42
Hornsey		12 48		12 56 12 56	1 4	1 11 1 12	1 18 1 18		1 26 1 28	1 31 1 31	1 32	1 41	1 45
Wood Green (Alex. Park)		12 51		12 59 12 59	1 7	1 14 1 16	1 21 1 23		1 29 1 31	1 34 1 34	1 35	1 44	1 48
Bowes Park				1 2	1 10			1 17	1 24 1 26	1 32	1 34	1 37 1 37	1 47
Palmer's Green & Southgate				1 5	1 13				1 27 1 29	1 37	1 37	1 40 1 40	1 50
Winchmore Hill				1 8	1 16				1 30 1 32	1 40	1 43 1 43	1 53
Grange Park				1 10	1 18				1 32 1 34	1 26 1 29	1 45 1 45	1 55
Enfield				1 13	1 21				1 35 1 37	1 31	1 48 1 48	1 58
GORDON HILL				1 16	1 23				1 38 1 40	1 33	1 58 1 53	
Crews Hill					1 30						1 57 1 57	
CUFFLEY & Goff's Oak ... arr.					1 34						2 1 2 1	
New Southgate ... dep.			12 55	1 3		1 12				1 28		1 39	1 53
Oakleigh Park			1 0	1 8		1 17				1 33		1 44	1 59
NEW BARNET			1 2	1 11		1 19				1 36		1 46	2 2
Hadley Wood				1 15				1 24		1 40			2 6
Potters Bar				1 19				1 29		1 45			2 10
HATFIELD ... arr.								1 36			
St. Albans (G.N.)								2 7			
Hertford								2 16			
Luton								2 36			
Dunstable (G.N.)								2 51			
HATFIELD ... dep.								1 38			
Welwyn			1 14					1 53			
Knebworth			1 19					2 0			
Stevenage			1 25					2 10			
HITCHIN ... arr.			1 31					2 16			
CAMBRIDGE			2 14								

Saturdays only. / *Saturdays excepted.* (annotations in various columns)

For notes and references see page 56.

NOTES: The numerous mid-day homegoing 'Saturdays only' trains, including one non-stop to Welwyn North, reflect the extent of Saturday morning working at that time. Aldersgate renamed Barbican 1 December 1968.

Appendix B4

Timetable of Up Services from Hitchin to Kings Cross in October 1943

(Reproduced from Bradshaws Timetable)

L·N·E·R   **855a**

Table 8a—*continued*   **HITCHIN, HATFIELD, and LONDON**

Week Days

	mrn	mrn	mrn	mrn	mrn	mrn	mrn					mrn	mrn		mrn	mrn					mrn	mrn		mrn	mrn			mrn	mrn	mrn
Hitchin.........dep		5 8	5 54	..	6 27	6 59	..	..	7 0	7 20	..	7 36	7 57	..	..	..	..	8 20	..	8 35	..	..	9 19
Stevenage........		5 17	6 2	..	6 35	6 59	..	..	7 9	7 28	..	7 44	8 5	..	..	..	..	8 28	..	8 43	..	..	9 27
Knebworth........		5 25	6 10	..	6 43	7 7	..	..	7 17	7 36	..	7 52	8 13	..	..	..	..	8 36	..	8 51	..	..	9 35
Welwyn North.....		5 32	6 17	..	6 51	7 15	..	..	7 25	7 43	..	8 0	8 21	..	..	..	..	8 44	..	8 58	..	..	9 42
Welwyn Garden City	4 50	5 36	6 21	6 49	6 56	7 20	..	7 10	7 27	7 30	7 47	7 48	8 6	8 25	..	8 33	8 46	8 49	8 55	9 5	..	9 37	9 47
Hatfield {arr	4 56	5 42	6 27	6 55	..	7 19	7 35	7 37	..	7 56	8 12	..	..	..	8 39	8 55	..	9 1	9 ..	9 45	..	
Hatfield {dep	4 58	5 49	6 29	6 58	..	7 13	7 24	..	7 38	..	8 28	14	..	8 18	8 40	..	..	9 29	11	9 20	..	
Finsbury Park..arr	5 40	6 31	6 58	7 35	7 22	7 44	7 54	7 52	..	8 3	8 18	8 33	8 39	8 49	8 56	9 21	..	9 16	9 39	9 35	10 1	..	1013
London (King's C)arr	5 47	6 38	7 3	7 42	7 29	7 51	8	2 7	7 59	..	8 10	8 18	8 40	8 47	8 56	9 29	..	9 23	..	9 42	10 9	..	1020

Week Days—*continued*

	mrn	mrn	mrn	mrn	mrn	mrn	S	E	S	aft	S	S	S	S	aft	S	aft	aft	S	aft	aft	aft	aft
Hitchin.........dep	9 32	10 8	1026	11 5	..	1116	..	..	..	1157	..	1235	..	1 50	..	1 58	..	..	2 54	..	..	4 9
Stevenage........	9 41	..	1034	..	..	1124	..	..	..	12 5	..	1243	..	..	..	2 6	..	..	3 2	..	..	4 16
Knebworth........	9 49	..	1042	..	..	1131	..	..	..	1212	..	1251	..	2 19	..	..	..	3 9	..	..	4 23
Welwyn North.....	9 56	..	1050	..	..	1138	..	..	..	1219	..	1259	..	..	..	2 26	..	3 17	..	..	4 29
Welwyn Garden City	10 0	..	1055	..	..	1143	..	1216	1219	1225	..	..	1 5	2 31	3 15	3 22	..	4 12	416	4 34
Hatfield {arr	10 6	11 1	11 1	..	1149	..	1222	1227	1231	..	..	0 2	37	3 23	3 28	..	4 20	424	4 40
Hatfield {dep	1013	..	11 3	..	1126	1150	1156	1220	1223	..	1232	1255	14	1 45	..	2 39	2 55	3 29	3 35	..	4 51
Finsbury Park..arr	1055	1046	1125	1144	12 7	1212	1238	1252	6	1252	..	1	8	1 58	2 25	3 2	3 40	3 53	4 16	5 25
London(King'sC)arr	11 1	1054	1133	1151	1214	1220	1248	..	1259	..	8	36	2 10	..	2 42	..	3 9	3 53	4 0	4 23	5 34

Week Days—*continued*

	aft	E	S	E	E	aft	aft	aft	aft	aft	E	aft	aft	aft	aft	aft	aft	aft	aft	S	E
Hitchin.........dep	4 24	4 42	..	..	5 15	5 20	..	5 57	..	6 30	..	..	7 41	8 31	..	8 51	..	9 46	1042	..
Stevenage........	..	4 50	..	..	5 23	5 28	..	6 38	..	6 38	..	7 49	..	8 58	..	9 55	1051	..
Knebworth........	..	4 58	..	..	535	540	..	6 12	..	6 46	..	7 57	..	9 6	..	10 4	11 0	..
Welwyn North.....	..	5 4	..	..	425	47	..	..	6 53	..	8 4	..	9 14	..	1011	11 7	..
Welwyn Garden City	4 35	8	..	5 41	475	53	6 12	..	6 30	6 35	58	7 25	7 32	..	8 9	8 24	919	..	1016	1112	..
Hatfield {arr	..	5 14	..	..	5 47	535	59	6 19	..	6 37	6 41	7	473	7 33	744	..	8 15	..	8 30	9 25	..	1022	1118
Hatfield {dep	..	5 15	5 14	5 28	5 49	5 55	1	..	6 24	..	648	7 8	..	7 47	8 17	..	8 34	9 33	9 48	1024	1120
Finsbury Park..arr	8 5	5 39	5 55	6	9 6	13	6 20	6 24	..	7 3	..	7 30	7 34	..	8 28	8 42	9 9	16	9 58	1029	11 0	1156
London(King'sC)arr	5 18	5 46	6	2	..	6 21	6 28	6 33	..	7 11	..	7 37	7 42	..	8 35	8 49	9 19	9 24	10 8	1038	11 8	12 4

Sundays

	mrn	mrn	mrn	mrn	mrn	mrn	mrn	mrn	mrn	mrn	mrn	aft	aft	aft	aft
Hitchin.........dep	..	6 1	..	..	7 36	..	9 36	..	1030	1044	..	..	1236	..	2 0	3 3
Stevenage........	..	6 10	..	..	7 45	..	8 35	9 45	..	1038	1053	..	..	1245	..	2 8	3 12
Knebworth........	..	622	..	..	7 54	..	8 43	9 54	..	1046	11 2	..	..	1254	..	2 16	3 20
Welwyn North.....	..	6 30	..	..	8 2	..	8 50	10 2	..	1053	1110	..	..	1 2	..	2 24	3 27
Welwyn Garden City	5 0	6 35	7 13	7 58	8 7	..	8 55	10 7	..	1058	1115	1125	..	1 7	..	2 29	3 32
Hatfield {arr	5 6	6 41	7 18	5 5	8 13	..	9 1	1013	11 4	..	1121	1131	..	1 15	..	2 35	3 38
Hatfield {dep	5 7	6 43	7 20	5 9	8 17	25	..	9 4	1018	11 6	..	1124	1135	1225	1 20	..	2 37	3 40
Finsbury Park..arr	5 48	7 24	8 1	7	419	6	9 36	..	1059	1132	..	1147	1216	1 62	3	3 16	4 6
London(King'sC)arr	5 55	7 31	8 8	..	8 48	9 13	..	9 45	11 8	..	1139	1156	1223	1 13	2 10	3 23	413

Sundays—*continued*

	aft	aft	aft	aft	aft	aft	aft	aft	aft	aft	aft	aft	aft	aft	aft	aft
Hitchin.........dep	..	..	5 3	5 38	5	..	..	6 36	7 1	7 58	8 39	..	9 28	9 45	9 53	..
Stevenage........	..	..	5 12	..	..	..	6 45	..	8 7	8 39	..	9 54	..	..
Knebworth........	..	..	5 20	..	..	..	6 54	..	8 16	8 53	..	10 8	..	..
Welwyn North.....	..	..	5 27	..	..	7 2	..	8 24	9 0	..	1016	..	..
Welwyn Garden City	..	..	5 32	5 55	24	..	7 37	7	..	8 29	9 5	..	1021	..	..
Hatfield {arr	..	..	5 38	6	1	..	7 10	7 13	..	8 35	9 11	..	1026	..	1040
Hatfield {dep	3 45	42	5 425	526	8	..	648	7 16	..	8 37	9 14	9 20	1035	..	1040
Finsbury Park..arr	4 26	513	6	446	336	306	50	7 26	8 3	7	419	16	9 44	16 1	10 8	1058	1032	1121
London(King'sC)arr	433	20	6 13	443	386	58	7 34	8 12	7 51	9 24	9 52	10 9	1018	11 6	1040	1128

‡ Change at Finsbury Park.   E or **E** Except Saturdays.   ‖ Arr. 4 mins. *earlier.*
S Saturdays only.   ‖ Arr. 5 mins. *earlier.*   Y Arr. 741 aft. on Saturdays.
Z Arr. 6 mins. *earlier.*   **A** Third class only.

For Intermediate Stations between Hatfield and King's Cross, see Suburban Time Table, page 1071.

NOTE: Despite the Second World War, the 1943 services were the most frequent to have been provided
for Welwyn North passengers up to that time.

Evening Peak Period London to Hertford and Hitchin Section of BR Kings Cross Suburban Timetable Commencing 6 March 1967

		Z								C				Z	A												C	
MOORGATE	d	..	..		1637	..		..	1650			1658	..		..				..	1707				..	1718				1731
ALDERSGATE	d	..	..		39	..		..	52			1702	..		..				..	09				..	20				33
FARRINGDON	d	..	..		41	..		..	54			04	..		..				..	11				..	24				35
KING'S CROSS	d	1641	....		1647	....		1655	....	1701		1710	1710		1714	1719		....	1717	1723				....	1730		1735		1739 1741
BROAD STREET	d	....	..		1641	..		..	1655		1705		..		1711			..	..		1715	..	1724						
DALSTON JUNCTION	d	....			46	....		..	1700		....		..		16			..			20	....	29						
FINSBURY PARK	a	46	..		52	..		52	1700		07	07	..	16	16		..	23	23				26	36	36	40			47
FINSBURY PARK	d	47	..		53	..		53	01		08	08	..	17	17		..	24	24				27	37	37	44			48
HARRINGAY WEST	d	..	..		..	..		56	..		11	..	..	20				..	27				..	..	47	..			
HORNSEY	d	..	..		..	..		59	..		13	..	..	22				..	29				..	..	47	..			
WOOD GREEN (ALEXANDRA PARK)	d	..	..		..	..		1702	..		16	..	..	25				..	32				32	..	50				
BOWES PARK	d										15			28									35	..	53				
PALMERS GREEN & SOUTHGATE	d							..	09		17			31									38	..	45	55			
WINCHMORE HILL	d							..	12		20			34									41	..	48	58			
GRANGE PARK	d							..	14		22	..	27	36									43	..	50	1800			
ENFIELD CHASE	d							..	17		25	..	29	38									45	..	52	03			
GORDON HILL	d							..	19		27	..	32	1742									48	..	55	05			
CREWS HILL	d							..	23					36									51	..	58	09			
CUFFLEY & GOFF'S OAK	d							..	27		1734			40									55	..	1803	13			
BAYFORD	d							..	32					45									1801	..	08				
HERTFORD NORTH	a				17d18			..	1739				1752							..	17d57		1807		1815	1823			
NEW SOUTHGATE & FRIERN BARNET	d							05			20								36					44						56
OAKLEIGH PARK	d							09			24								40					48	..					1800
NEW BARNET	d				1704			12			26							35	43					51						1803
HADLEY WOOD	d				07			15			30							39	1746		1746			54						
POTTERS BAR & SOUTH MIMMS	d				11			19			34							1746		42	51			59						
BROOKMAN'S PARK	d				15			24			38									46	55		1803							
HATFIELD	a	1706			20			29			1743								1752	1800		1810								
HATFIELD	d	07			21			30								1744				01									
WELWYN GARDEN CITY	a	11			1727			1736								44	1749			1808									
WELWYN GARDEN CITY	d	12			..			..								45				..									
WELWYN NORTH	d	..			..			..							42					..								1807	
KNEBWORTH	d	21			..			..								54				..									
STEVENAGE	d	27	34		..			..							53	1800				1813							16		
HITCHIN	a	1733	1741		..			..			1749			1759	1806												1821		

NOTE: The timetable includes two non-stop trains from Kings Cross to Welwyn North, the second with a buffet car.

Appendix B6

The Mondays to Fridays Royston to Kings Cross Section of the First Great Northern Electrics Outer Suburban Timetable Commencing 6 February 1978

Royston	d.	05 35	06 05	06 32	07 02	07 15	07 22	07 35	07 42	07 56	08 05	08 10	08 25	08 35	08 55	08 58	09 32	09 35
Ashwell & Morden	d.	05 40	06 10	06 37	07 07		07 27		07 47	08 01		08 15		08 40			09 03	09 40
Baldock	d.	05 45	06 15	06 42	07 12		07 32		07 52	08 06		08 20		08 45			09 08	09 45
Letchworth	d.	05 49	06 19	06 46	07 16	07 25	07 36	07 45	07 56	08 10	08 15	08 24	08 35	08 49	09 05	09 10	09 12	09 49
Hitchin	d.	05 53	06 23	06 50	07 20	07 30	07 40	07 50	08 00	08 15	08 20	08 28	08 40	08 53	09 10	09 16	09 49	09 53
Stevenage	d.	05 59	06 29	06 56	07 26	07 35	07 46	07 55	08 06	08 20	08 25	08 34	08 45	08 59	09 22	09 22	09 54	09 59
Knebworth	d.	06 03	06 33	07 00	07 30		07 50		08 10		08 29	08 38		09 03		09 26		10 03
Welwyn North	d.	06 07	06 37	07 04	07 34		07 54		08 14		08 34	08 42		09 07		09 30		10 07
Welwyn Garden City	d.	06 10	06 40	07 07	07 37		07 57		08 17			08 45		09 10		09 33		10 10
Hatfield	d.	06 13	06 43											09 13		09 36		10 13
Potters Bar	d.	06 19	06 49											09 19		09 42		10 19
Finsbury Park	a.	06 29	06 59	07 23	07 53	07 58	08 13	08 18	08 33	08 42	08 53	09 00	09 05	09 29		09 56	10 22	10 29
King's Cross	a.	06 36	07 06	07 29	08 00	08 04	08 20	08 2+	08 40	08 49	09 00	09 05	09 11	09 36	10 03	10 22	10 36

Royston	d.	10 05	10 32	10 35		17 05	17 35	18 02	18 05	19 05	19 32	19 35	20 05	20 35	23 05
Ashwell & Morden	d.	10 10		10 40		17 10	17 40		18 10	19 10		19 40	20 10	20 40	23 10
Baldock	d.	10 15		10 45		17 15	17 45		18 15	19 15		19 45	20 15	20 45	23 15
Letchworth	d.	10 19	10 42	10 49		17 19	17 49	18 12	18 19	19 19	19 42	19 49	20 19	20 49	23 19
Hitchin	d.	10 23	10 47	10 53		17 23	17 53	18 17	18 23	19 23	19 47	19 53	20 23	20 53	23 23
Stevenage	d.	10 29	10 52	10 59		17 29	17 59	18 25	18 22	19 04	19 29	19 52	19 59	20 29	20 59	23 29
Knebworth	d.	10 33		11 03		17 33	18 03		18 33	19 08	19 33		20 03	21 03	23 33
Welwyn North	d.	10 37		11 07		17 37	18 07		18 37	19 12	19 37		20 07	21 07	23 37
Welwyn Garden City	d.	10 40		11 10		17 40	18 10		18 40	19 15	19 40		20 10	21 10	23 40
Hatfield	d.	10 43		11 13		17 43	18 13		18 43	19 18	19 43		20 13	21 13	23 43
Potters Bar	d.	10 49		11 19		17 49	18 19		18 49	19 24	19 49		20 19	21 19	23 49
Finsbury Park	a.	10 59		11 29		17 59	18 29	18 50	18 59	19 34	19 59		20 29	21 29	23 58
King's Cross	a.	11 06	11 20	11 36		18 06	18 36	18 56	19 06	19 41	20 12	20 20	20 36	21 06	21 36	00 06

and at the same minutes past each hour until (D)

and at the same minutes past each hour until (C)

Appendix B7

Morning Peak Period Huntingdon and Royston to Stevenage and Royston to Stevenage and London Section of the ABC Rail Guide October 1985

(Reproduced by kind permission of Reed Telepublishing Ltd.)

Mondays to Fridays

Peterborough	dp	0250	0310	0319	0329	0334				0516 0531					0647 0705 0714 0723 0729		0702 0735 0740 0745 0750 0755
Huntingdon	dp	0317 (MO)	0317 (MX)						0555			0627 0644 0653 0703 0708				
St. Neots		0723 0744 0749													0705 0714	
Sandy															0723	
Biggleswade															0729	
Cambridge 102	dp	0724														0702

Royston		0730 0745	0751 0759 0808 0814			0555 0625 0630 0635 0640 0650	0653 0701 0708 0714 0718	0425 0430 0435 0440 0445 0450	0709 0714 0721 0724 0728 0734	0728 0736 0742	0732 0736 0742	0753 0757 0801	0735 0740 0745 0750 0755	0802 0808 0815 0820
Ashwell & Morden														
Baldock						0554	0722 0726 0730				0746 0750 0754		
Letchworth						0558 0602	0733 0739		0801 0812		0758		
Hitchin						0605 0611 0624 0628 0632	0751 0804 0806 0822		0719 0742 0759 0725	0833 0822			
Stevenage						0635 0641 0647 0652			0731 0742 0759 0725		0757 0812 0803	0820 0833 0825 0813	
Watton-at-Stone						0701 0712 0725 0729			0729				
Hertford North	ar												
Knebworth													
Welwyn North													
Welwyn Garden City													
Hatfield 100													
Potters Bar 100													
Finsbury Park 100													
Moorgate 100	ar												
King's Cross 100	ar												

Mondays to Fridays—contd

Peterborough	dp						0814	0845			0855 0905	0913 0922 0932 0937	0925 0930 0935 0940 0950 0953	0942 0947 0952 0957 1007
Huntingdon	dp					0806 0811 0816 0820 0825 0831	0835	0825 0830 0835 0844 0850 0856	0836 0854 0903 0913 0919	0905 0941 0930 0935 0958		
St. Neots		0754 0759 0804	0806 0811 0816 0822	0816 0820 0825 0834 0839		0855 0902	0910 0914 0924 0930 0948 0953	0924 0928 0932 0942 0943 0950	0951 1007	0954 0958 1002	
Sandy		0809 0819 0825			0826 0830 0834				0943		
Biggleswade					0835 0839 0843	0835 0839 0843	0846 0854 0904 0910				
Cambridge 102	dp				0846 0855 0901	0857		0901	0910		1035 1041 1047 1035	1126 1137 1158

Royston	dp	0715 0730 0737	0751 0759 0808 0814	0806 0809 0816 0819 0825			0835 0839 0843	0846 0854 0904 0910	0905 0941 0907 0923	0915 0953 0958	0925 0930 0935 0940 0950 0953	1010 1014 1020 1024 1030 1035	1126 1137 1158
Ashwell & Morden												
Baldock		0725 0744 0749										
Letchworth			0803 0811 0825						0951			
Hitchin		0754 0758 0804	0808 0813 0819	0812 0816 0820 0824 0831			0844 0855 0909			1006 1008		
Stevenage		0808 0817	0819 0823	0826 0830 0834				0837 0846 0855		1024 1028 1032		
Watton-at-Stone				0802 0808 0815 0820				0847 0900 0901				
Hertford North	ar											
Knebworth											1035 1041		
Welwyn North												
Welwyn Garden City		0817	0820 0826 0833 0836 0843	0813 0824 0836 0843			0902 0909		1008			
Hatfield 100												
Potters Bar 100												
Finsbury Park 100		0830	0854 0858 0902									
Moorgate 100	ar	0817	0819 0854	0817								
King's Cross 100	ar											

MO Mondays only
MX Mondays excepted

NOTE: The 0801 from Welwyn North, introduced May 1985, became that station's most used train.

Appendix C

Welwyn North's Record Trains

1 The Fastest Trains

From Welwyn North to Kings Cross (22 miles)
The 0805 departure in the May 1986 timetable was allowed 23 minutes (average speed 57.4 mph) for the journey including one stop at Finsbury Park.

From Welwyn North to Finsbury Park (19 miles 39 chains)
The 0805 departure in the May 1986 timetable was scheduled to make this journey non-stop in 17 minutes (average speed 68.8 mph). The timing was intended for the Class 317/2 Electric Multiple Units (max. speed 100 mph). However the slower Class 312 units have been severally recorded as having completed the journey in 14¾ minutes (average speed 79.3 mph). The Class 312 units were allowed 19 minutes for this journey in the 1981/2 and 1985/6 timetables (average speed 61.5 mph).

From Kings Cross to Welwyn North
The 1804 departure in 1971–2, formed by a Diesel Multiple Unit, was scheduled to run non-stop between the two stations in 26 minutes (average speed 50.8 mph). Between 1978 and 1981 the same time was allowed for several peak period trains, formed by Class 312 EMUs, which had two intermediate stops at Finsbury Park and Welwyn Garden City.

The performance of the various non-stop services was as follows:

Year	Time of departure from Kings Cross	Time allowed to Welwyn North (mins)	Average speed (mph)	Notes
1919	12.40 pm	34	38.8	Saturdays only
1967/8	1714	28	47.1	
1967/8	1739	28	47.1	Buffet Car
1971/2	1804	26	50.8	
1977/8	1722	28	47.1	

2 The Slowest Trains

From Welwyn North to Kings Cross
In 1850 the all stations 9.18 am departure from Welwyn was scheduled to arrive at Maiden Lane (21 miles 22 chains) at 11 am (average speed 12.5 mph).
In 1935 the 6.33 pm all stations, except Hornsey and Harringay West, was allowed 77 minutes being due to arrive in Kings Cross at 7.50 pm (average speed 17.1 mph). This train was not passed by any alternative faster services.
In 1959 the 5.28 am was allowed 64 minutes for its all stations journey to Kings Cross (average speed 20.6 mph).

From Kings Cross to Welwyn North
From 1887 to 1921 the first down train to Welwyn departed from Kings Cross at 7 am and called at all stations before arriving at Welwyn 76 minutes later at 8.16 am (average speed 17.4 mph) and continuing to Cambridge.
In September 1935 the 3.30 pm from Kings Cross took 98 minutes to reach Welwyn North (average speed 13.5 mph). This was largely due to a long wait at Hatfield to allow passengers on a following fast train to connect with it.
In December 1959 the 6.53 am Kings Cross to Cambridge took 63 minutes to reach Welwyn North (average speed 21.0 mph).

3 Other fast and unusual trains

In 1852 the 6 am from Retford to London ran non-stop from Hitchin to Welwyn (9 miles 74 chains) where it arrived at 9.53 am. It took 18 minutes for this part of its journey.
Since Knebworth opened in 1884 it has been normal for trains to and from Welwyn North to call at both stations. There have, however, been a few exceptions. For example, in 1887 the 3.18 pm from Welwyn ran non-stop to Stevenage. More recently in 1967/8, the 1714 and 1739 departures from Kings Cross ran non-stop to Welwyn North and from there to Stevenage (then 6 miles 46 chains from Welwyn North).
Until the mid-1930s particularly on Sundays, some trains, averaging less than 30 mph, called at most stations between Kings Cross and York (188 miles) which remains the furthest destination of trains that have called at Welwyn North (166 miles).
Prior to electrification in 1978 there were several trains daily from Welwyn North to Cambridge (35 miles 75 chains), one to Huntingdon (36 miles 70 chains) and at weekends, one to Peterborough (54 miles 29 chains).
In 1986 the longest direct journeys possible at Welwyn North are to Royston (22 miles 72 chains) and from Moorgate (22 miles 69 chains). By travelling on the 0802 from Welwyn North in 1985/6 and changing at Stevenage, travellers could be in Wakefield (153 miles 67 chains), in 106 minutes (average speed 88.7 mph).
In 1914 the 3.1 pm, Sundays only, terminated at Knebworth (only 3 miles 3 chains).
There have been at least three up services calling at Welwyn North which terminated at Welwyn Garden City (only 1 mile 55 chains).

Principal Sources and References

Anon (1864) Great Northern Railway: Digswell Viaduct. *Record of Modern Engineering* 1864:31–32.

Anon (1864) Great Northern Railway: Robbery Wood Viaduct. *Record of Modern Engineering* 1864:32.

Borley, H. V. (1973) The Hertford, Luton & Dunstable Railway. *Journal of the Railway & Canal Historic Society* 19:48–50.

Busby, R. J. (1976) *The Book of Welwyn*. Barracuda Books, Chesham.

Clarke, A. M. (1975) The Welwyn Garden City Light Railway. *Industrial Railway Record* 6:97–102.

Cockman, F. G. (2nd edn 1983) *The Railways of Hertfordshire*. Hertford.

Fellows, R. B. (1937) London & Hertford. *Railway Magazine* 80:143–4.

Fellows, R. B. (1976) *London to Cambridge by Train 1845–1938*. The Oleander Press, Cambridge.

Foster, A. M. (1981) *The Book of Hitchin*. Barracuda Books, Chesham.

Fry, E. V. (Ed 1963–85). *Locomotives of the L.N.E.R.* (9 Parts). Railway Correspondence and Travel Society.

Gladwin, T. W., Neville, P. W. and White, D. E. (1985) *Welwyn North: The Story of the Railway*. Published privately.

Gladwin, T. W. and Sage, B. L. (1986) *The Birds of Hertfordshire*. Castlemead, Ware.

Goode, C. T. (1984) *The Hertford Loop Line*. The Oakwood Press, Shaftesbury.

Grinling, C. H. (rev. edn 1966). *The History of the Great Northern Railway 1845–1922*. Allen & Unwin, London.

Hatfield Workers' Educational Association. (1960) *Hatfield and its People: Part 5 Roads and Railways*.

Hertfordshire County Council. (1980) *Public Transport Plan 1980–81*.

Hertfordshire County Council. (1984) *Public Transport Plan 1984/5 to 1988/9*.

Hodge, P. (1976) *The Hertford Loop*. Southgate Civic Trust.

Jackson, A. A. (1978) *London's Local Railways*. David & Charles, Newton Abbot.

Johns, C. A. (1939) The 5.5 p.m. from Kings Cross. *Railway Magazine* 84:235–236.

Knebworth Workers' Educational Association. (3rd edn 1967) *Knebworth: The Story of Our Village*.

Morel, J. (1983) *Pullman*. David & Charles, Newton Abbot.

Neve, E. (1977) The Great Northern Route to Cambridge. *Railway World* 38:446–450, 493–497.

Neve, E. (1983) *East Coast from Kings Cross*. Ian Allan, Shepperton.

Neve, E. (1985) East Coast Main Line Traffic Survey – 1984. *Railway Observer* 55:35–36, 139.

Neve, E. (1986) Seeing how they ran in 1985. *Railway World* 47:95–102.

Newman, J. C. (1974) Railway Signal Boxes on the Great Northern Line – a valediction. *Hertfordshire Countryside* 29:32–34.

Ottley, G. (2nd edn 1983) *A Bibliography of British Railway History*. HMSO, London.

Percival, D. (1984) *Kings Cross Lineside 1958–1984*. Ian Allan, Shepperton.

Robert, R. (1962) Brassey Builds the Viaduct. *Hertfordshire Countryside* 17:200–201.

Semmens, P. W. B., Perren, B., and Porter, W. A. (1977) *Quest for Speed*. British Rail Eastern Region.

Thrower, W. R. (1978) *King's Cross in the Twenties*. The Oakwood Press, Blandford.

Thrower, W. R. (1984) *The Great Northern Main Line*. The Oakwood Press, Shaftesbury.

Ward, D. (1953) *Digswell from Domesday to Garden City*. Welwyn & District Regional Survey Association, Welwyn Garden City.

White, H. P. (1963) *A Regional History of the Railways of Great Britain vol. 3 – Greater London*. David & Charles, Newton Abbot.

Williams, A. (1967) Welwyn North. *Model Railway Constructor* Feb 1967.

Woodward, G. and S. (1977) *The Hatfield, Luton & Dunstable Railway*. The Oakwood Press, Blandford.

Wrottesley, J. (1979–81) *The Great Northern Railway*. (3 vols). Batsford, London.

Young, J. N. (1977) *Great Northern Suburban*. David & Charles, Newton Abbot.

Journals and periodicals

Great Northern Railway Society Newsletters
Hertfordshire Countryside
Illustrated London News
London & North Eastern Railway Magazine
Modern Railways
Railway Magazine
Railway Observer
Railway Official Timetables
Railway World
The Times
Welwyn and Hatfield Times

Index